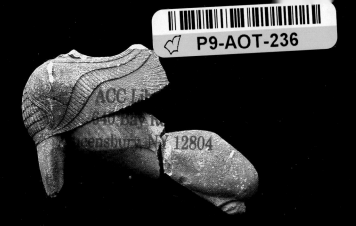

or, more precisely, a science that has its own rules.
Those rules were not really formulated until the
second half of the 19th century. Excavations by
inexperienced archaeologists, without the aid of
trained architects, were carried out for the sole
purpose of gathering and putting into a safe place
as many movable objects and trinkets as possible –
bearing an uncanny resemblance to organized
burglary. It is, therefore, better that Greece has
abstained from premature and, hence, risky ventures;
after all, the earth that covers the ruins is a good
shield. **"**

Théodore Reinach, president of the Association for the
Encouragement of Greek Studies in France
Greece Returned to the Greeks, 1907

CONTENTS

THE SEARCH FOR ANCIENT GREECE

Roland and Françoise Etienne

Thames & Hudson

12

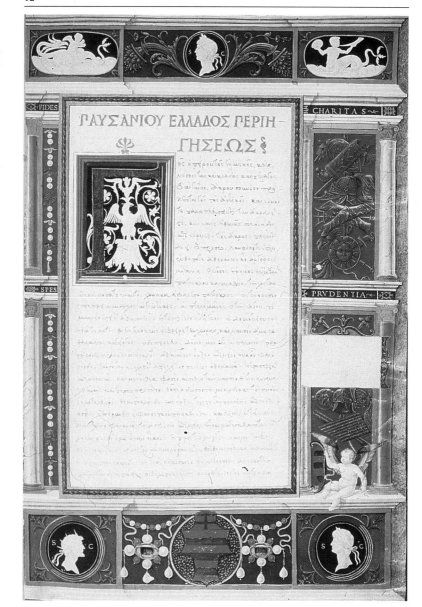

> **"Cato predicted that the Romans would lose their empire when they had gorged themselves on Greek literature. But time has proved the vanity of that sacrilegious prediction, since Rome attained the summit of her prosperity at the very moment when she was appropriating for herself Greek science and Greek culture as a whole."**
>
> Plutarch, 2nd century AD

CHAPTER 1

ROME INVENTS GREECE

The *Doryphoros (Spear Bearer)*, a statue often copied, was one of the masterpieces of Polyclitos (460–420 BC). On the right is a copy of its head by the Athenian sculptor Apollonios, the son of Archias, as the inscription tells us (1st century BC). Opposite: frontispiece of a late-15th century edition of Pausanias.

If archaeologists began working in Greece a long time ago, it was largely because classical Greek civilization had been lionized for so long. The process began in the 5th century BC and was already flourishing in the Hellenistic period, that is, from the 3rd century BC until the 2nd century AD.

The conquest of the Persian empire by

These three statues are Roman copies of Greek originals. They come from the Villa dei Papyri in Herculaneum, where a set of thirty-eight sculptures was found, including the *Doryphoros* on the previous page. It has been deduced from texts written on papyri found in the house that its owner, Lucius Calpurnius Piso Caesonius, was a disciple of Epicurus. He brought together an amazing array of copies of famous statues to evoke the end of the 4th and early 3rd centuries BC, when Epicurus was alive.

 Opposite: an archaic-style Athena Promachos ready for combat.

Left: a bronze possibly representing a Danaid.

Below: this bronze of Hermes resting was for a long time attributed to Lysippos (340–310 bc).

Alexander the Great (starting in 334 BC) and the founding of kingdoms controlled by Greeks throughout the eastern Mediterranean had three notable effects: the creation of a culture based on the works of Homer; the beginning of art collecting; and a rudimentary sort of art history, which classified works and evaluated their creators. Greek rulers certainly had the means to employ artists and to buy works of art, and they did not hesitate to acquire the finest pieces for themselves.

Following this example, the Romans, who had grown wealthy through the exploitation of most of the inhabited world, in their turn developed collections and took part in the celebration and pillage of classical Greece from the middle of the 2nd century BC.

During the first two centuries of the

Roman empire, for different reasons and with more or less discretion, emperors like Augustus, Nero and Hadrian shared the Republican elite's taste for things Greek. Augustus and Hadrian both had reproductions made of the caryatids (six female figures) of the Erechtheion, the former for his Forum in Rome, the latter for his villa at Tivoli.

Pausanias writes the first guidebook

By the 2nd century AD, Greece had already become a museum; Pausanias, a Greek traveller and geographer who worked from AD 143 to 176, devoted ten books to it. In his *Description of Greece*, he invites his readers to accompany him on a tour of all the interesting sites, thereby setting the format for subsequent writings on travel. Such writings remained the most important means of discovering Greece until the 19th century. Pausanias is extremely important, even if he was not the first or the only person to have composed this kind of guide. His work is the only complete one of its kind to have survived. It was with Pausanias in hand that serious travellers of the 18th and 19th centuries explored the riches of Greece.

Was Pausanias a reliable guide? He has been much

In the illustration below for a 1731 edition of Pausanias, the artist has drawn, with a degree of imagination, the hippodrome of Olympia during the great competitions. Pausanias reveals few details about himself. A Greek from Asia Minor, he must have come from a wealthy family to have been able to travel as he did from the Euphrates valley to Italy.

maligned, yet where the information he gives can be checked, it is very often correct. It was thanks to Pausanias that the sanctuary of the Boeotian Confederation at Onchestos was recently identified and excavated. Despite his accuracy, however, his seriousness and intelligence have been questioned, and he has been criticized for having no artistic taste of his own: he makes few judgments, preferring instead to describe and to inform. In the tradition of scholars since the 2nd century BC, he ranks the sculptor Phidias as the greatest of classical Greece and Alcamenes second. He has a respect for archaic works, and, by making comparisons, he is able to recognize the style of a great artist.

For his modesty, his desire to complete a difficult undertaking and his love of liberty and opposition to tyranny, Pausanias is a generally engaging character who, at the very least, brings to life the sites of ancient Greece.

Eighty years after Pausanias, part of Greece was ravaged by barbarians, and Athens was ransacked by the Herulians in AD 267. A gradual process of destruction – a result of the invasions and the increasing power of Christianity – provoked a shift of the centres of creativity; at the same time, changes in taste led people to forget, for a while, the monuments of Greece.

The *Description* deals with only part of Greece, and it is not possible to explain the omissions (Macedonia, Thrace, Aetolia, Acarnania and the islands). However, he describes the monuments in minute detail, gives a list of statues and describes the traditions he heard from local guides at all the sites he does visit. Pausanias' work was not highly appreciated in antiquity.

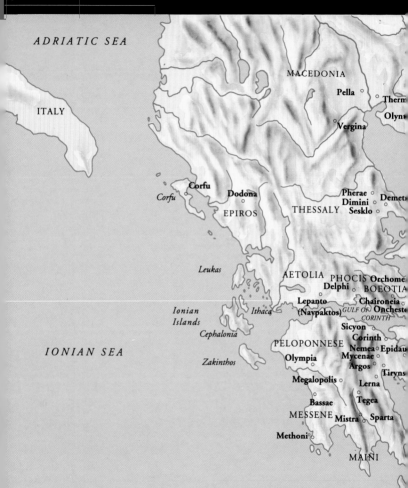

ADRIATIC SEA

MACEDONIA

Pella ○   ○ Therm

ITALY

Olyn

○ Vergina

Corfu   Dodona
Corfu   ○   Pherae ○   Demet
               EPIROS   THESSALY Dimini
                                      Seeklo ○

Leukas

AETOLIA PHOCIS Orchome
                Delphi ○ BOEOTIA

Ionian   Lepanto   Chaironeia ○
Islands   Ithaca (Naypaktos) GULF OF Onchest
        Cephalonia   CORINTH
                              Sicyon
IONIAN SEA   Corinth ○
                    PELOPONNESE Nemea ○ Epidau
               Zakinthos   Mycenae ○
                         Olympia Argos ○
                                         Tiryns
                         Megalopolis ○
                                      Lerna
                         Bassae   Tegea
                              MESSENE Mistra ○ Sparta
                         Methoni ○

                              MAINI

ANCIENT GREECE

THRACE

SEA OF
MARMARA

Amphipolis

Thasos

Samothrace

Troy   PHRYGIA

Lemnos

Northern
Sporades

Lesbos   Pergamum

Skyros

UBOEA   AEGEAN SEA

Chios

Eretria
Oropos
ebes   Rhamnos
eusis   Marathon   LYDIA
Athens   Samos   Ephesos
racus   Brauron
TICA   Sounion   Andros   Sporades   Miletos
legina   Tenos   CARIA
roezen   Kea
ydra   Kythnos   Delos
                    Southern
          Paros   Naxos   Sporades
          Cyclades   Amorgos   Kos

          Melos

          Thera   Dodecanese   Lindos
          (Santorini)   Rhodes

SEA OF CRETE   Karpathos

                    Mallia
          Knossos   0   100 km
CRETE   Lato
Phaistos   Gortyn   Kato Zakros

scias quibus in locis ampla pandebatur planities. Si aŭt ad trionem accedes sil
uam. et ãbrachium suum offendes. ad orientem deniq; insule monlte propa
lentur: in quibus olim habitauere patres: nunc tandem pp insidias pyrratarum
ad desolationem denenere:

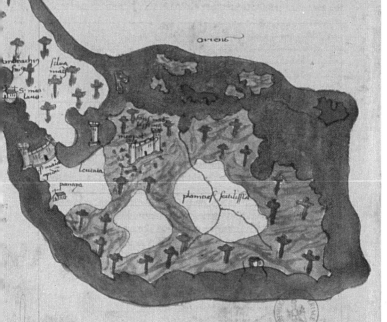

orion

brachiu
fori

silua
maii

mõt. s. mes
nuc laŭó

leuiam

panaya

plamies fertilissia

Ostendimus Leucatam nunc ad dulichias transimus que olis itacha et nunc
ual de compare nominatur. altis rupib; circumsepta. que montiosa est
innuilis: nisi in medio exiguus planicie a liquito arborib; casisq; habetur. et ric
cum circa poetiosa sate d oriente ad oriddium pppp. et in latitudine. vij mil.
amplatur. cuius quidem duo extrema induob; apertur cornib; a nautis in
noste periculosis. Fuit enim hunc ut asserunt ille eloquentissim̃ grecorum Ulyxes

> **"**I was driven by an ardent desire to see the world, to seek out those monuments of antiquity which have for so long been the principal object of my study, and to put down on paper those that are, day by day, falling into ruin because of the long assault of time and the carelessness of men, and which deserve to be remembered.**"**
>
> Cyriacus of Ancona, 1441

CHAPTER 2

CYRIACUS OF ANCONA, PIONEER OF ARCHAEOLOGY

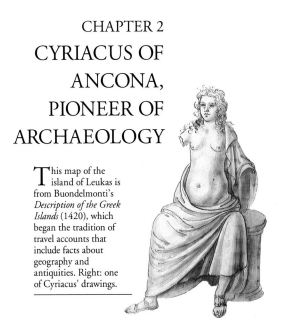

This map of the island of Leukas is from Buondelmonti's *Description of the Greek Islands* (1420), which began the tradition of travel accounts that include facts about geography and antiquities. Right: one of Cyriacus' drawings.

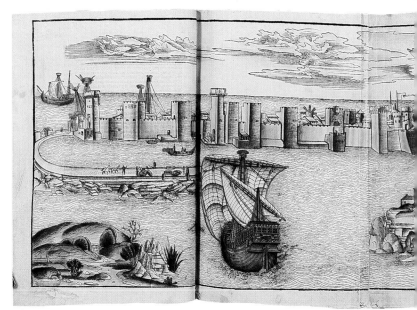

The Roman empire, which had been divided into eastern
and western empires in 285 by Diocletian and reunited
in 324 by Constantine, was divided again in 395. Greece
became a province of the eastern, or Byzantine, empire,
and the focal point of Greek life moved from Athens to
Constantinople.

A troubled period thus began for Greece, marked by
the invasions of the Slavic peoples from the 6th to the 9th
centuries. The invaders settled in Macedonia and Thrace
and adopted Greek customs partially and gradually.
Then the capture of Constantinople by the Crusaders in
1204 placed Greece under the control of the Franks,
feudal lords from western Europe.

Greece unrecognized

This event marked the beginning of a period of six
centuries during which the Greeks continually found
themselves ruled by foreign masters, masters whom they
tirelessly resisted.

Ancient Greece was never entirely forgotten, even in

The city of Methoni (located at the southern tip of Messenia, on a promontory jutting out into the sea), together with its neighbour, Koroni, formed part of the possessions given to the Venetians in the breakup of the Byzantine empire in 1204. Methoni was an important outpost of the Venetian empire and of its trade in the East, and Venice defended it jealously against all attacks by Greeks and Turks. It was also a port of call on the route to the Holy Land. The following account by an anonymous French pilgrim in 1480 dates from the same time as the drawing on these pages: 'Methoni is a strong city, well equipped with artillery and very well protected by walls. In front of the city there is a fine harbour, which can shelter galleys and ships, and it is surrounded by fine walls that break up the waves of the sea.'

the Middle Ages, but, as century followed century, it was less and less understood, for both religious and cultural reasons. The medieval Christian mind was, by definition, opposed to Hellenic culture (that is, Greek culture from 776 BC to 323 BC), which had become synonymous with paganism. The closing of the philosophical schools by the Emperor Justinian in the 6th century was as great a sign of the triumph of Christianity and the breaking with the ancient past as was the transformation of the temples into churches. The Parthenon was consecrated to the cult of the Virgin, and the 'Theseion' (a temple of Hephaistos erroneously thought to have been dedicated to Theseus), to Saint George. Christian Greeks for a long time called themselves Romans rather than Hellenes.

In the West, the Greek lands had aroused distrust and hostility ever since the separation of the Eastern Orthodox Church from the Roman Catholic Church in 1054. In the eyes of Pope Innocent III (c. 1160–1216) the Greeks were 'worse than the Saracens'. It was therefore without scruple that his Crusaders sacked

Constantinople and divided up the empire among themselves.

The conquerors only appeared to end the isolation of Greece. Traditionally, pilgrimage routes to Jerusalem and the trade routes to the Levant (the eastern Mediterranean) followed the southern coast of the Peloponnese, passing among the islands without going through the interior of the country. Charts called portolanos, in use from the 13th century, showed the outline of the coasts with some precision. Since the structures of the Acropolis could be seen from the port of Piraeus, Athens appears on these charts, but as Setines (a phonetic corruption of Athena). However, they provide little information about the interior of the country.

Pilgrims were interested only in religious remains and relics. Whether they crossed by land, at Corinth, or by sea, they did not make any detours from their route to see the remains of pagan idolatry.

The powerful trading ports of Genoa and Venice created their own spheres of influence: Genoa's was the northern Aegean and the Black Sea, Venice's the south, including Beirut and Alexandria. Continental Greece occupied a marginal position in relation to these great centres of commerce.

Greece rediscovered

At the turn of the 14th century, two pioneers in the rediscovery of Greece broke a silence that had lasted for centuries. They were Cristoforo Buondelmonti and Ciriaco de' Pizzicolli (Cyriacus of Ancona). Both were Italians, and both took part in the humanist movement that was flourishing in Italy. But humanism was almost exclusively concerned with the texts of ancient authors and with the search for manuscripts, whereas these two

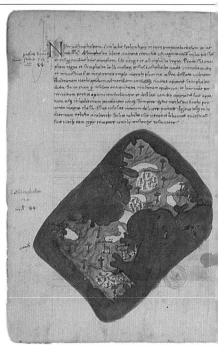

Buondelmonti's map of Astypalaia (above left) shows that although it is 'very narrow in the middle, this island is quite wide at each end, where there are ruins of several fortified towns.' Above right, Santorini: 'It was considered very fertile and densely populated but, being undermined by volcanic activity, one-half of it collapsed beneath the waves. We can see one of the portions of this island in the sea, charred and crescent-shaped. We call it Therasia.'

travellers were interested in actual places and in faithfully reproducing what they saw there. To Buondelmonti, a Florentine monk, we owe the first attempt at historical cartography to be applied to Greece. He visited the islands of the Aegean as a geographer and man of learning.

Cyriacus the merchant

The work of Cyriacus was broader and more diverse than that of Buondelmonti; Cyriacus can be considered the founder of archaeology. He was born in 1391 in Ancona, one of the most active and prosperous ports in Italy, to a family of merchants that specialized in trade over long distances.

As a travelling merchant representative of his class and time, Cyriacus was blessed with the spirit of enterprise. He had a taste for risk and a thirst for riches. Entrusted with diplomatic missions and various embassies for his government, he was in touch with influential people.

In Constantinople, in 1444, he was involved in the preparation of the crusade against the Turks. He had campaigned actively for this crusade, in part to win markets back from the Turks, but mainly with the idea of prolonging the life of the ancient world, which was under severe threat from the advancing Ottoman empire.

Like many Italian merchants of the 15th century, Cyriacus traded in manuscripts and small antiquities, which he bought in the Levant. He sold medals, coins and intaglios to rich collectors and art lovers for high prices. Among them was this precious intaglio in rock crystal representing Athena, on which Cyriacus deciphered an inscription in 1445 while on board a Venetian galley: 'Eutyches, the son of Diokourides, of Aigai, made this.'

Cyriacus the archaeologist

How was it that, at about the age of thirty, this shrewd merchant became a pioneer of archaeology? His education had not prepared him for the role – he had not attended a university – but his first voyages aroused his curiosity about the monuments of the past. Around 1420 he began copying inscriptions in Pola and in Rome. It was then that an idea occurred to him that was original for its time: that 'the monuments and inscriptions are more faithful witnesses of classical antiquity than are the texts of ancient writers.' He decided to gather all the testimony of antiquity that he encountered in his travels in one book. This was the *Commentary upon Ancient Things*, of which only a few fragments have been preserved.

It would be wrong to assume that a new life as a scholar and explorer began for Cyriacus with this book. He did not give up his trade; on the contrary, his commercial travels facilitated his archaeological explorations. Trade became the pretext for excursions into unfamiliar regions and for the exploration of abandoned cities to copy inscriptions and to draw the monuments.

From letters he wrote to his friends, we know that he

On this drawing of a relief of the Muses from Samothrace, Cyriacus inscribed the names of the Muses over the figures in Greek letters. It was not until later, when he was about forty, that he started to study ancient Greek. His knowledge of Latin remained imperfect and his style was weak and awkward. The practical training he had received was in geography, arithmetic and cartography.

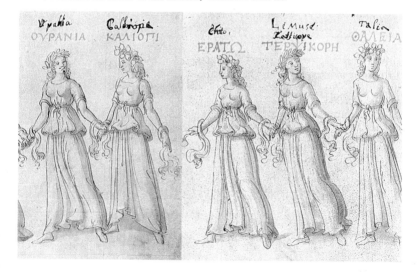

These documents come from Delos, where Cyriacus spent some time in 1445. His drawings are awkward and naive. The female sculpture with the long hair and the leg of the Colossus of the Naxians (far left) are only very rough sketches. By contrast, the depiction of the base of the Colossus with one foot in place (near left) is truer to life. All the inscriptions are painstakingly reproduced, even if they are incomplete. One can make out the dedication of the Naxians to Apollo, two offerings to King Mithradates of Pontos, and a consecration of Philip V of Macedon.

made scholarly preparations for his journeys. In addition to maps and portolanos, he used a number of works as guides: Ptolemy's *Geography*, Pliny's *Natural History*, and, at the end of his life, the work of Strabo, a Greek geographer who lived at about the time of Christ. He did not, however, own a manuscript copy of Pausanias – this is clear from his erroneous identifications of certain sites. Cyriacus was able to penetrate into Hellenic regions without any difficulty since he spoke the Greek of the day and had developed relationships with local potentates. In Athens he stayed at the court of the dukes of Acciaioli, and he spent a winter at the home of the despot of Mistra, where the Neoplatonist philosopher Gemistus Plethon was a teacher.

Cyriacus' great journey to Greece took place between 1434 and 1435. In the course of this and two subsequent trips, in 1444 and 1447 to 1448, Cyriacus visited almost all the regions that make up modern Greece.

Looking over Cyriacus' shoulder

The loss of most of the *Commentary* is irreparable; however, from the fragments of it that have been preserved and from his letters, one can form quite a clear idea of Cyriacus' methods.

The drawings of the material he saw at Delos are sometimes extremely precise, even if his readings of the inscriptions leave something to be desired, either because he read them badly or because the originals were difficult to decipher. But in spite of the scope of his epigraphic work, he was by no means over scrupulous and did not hesitate to produce fakes.

The authenticity of the oracles he is supposed to have copied at Delphi is questionable; except for a few variants, they are the same as those given by Herodotus, so he probably took them from the great historian rather than from Delphi. Similarly, he claimed to have read some short poems on stone; in fact, these were epigrams he had borrowed from Maximus Planudes' *Anthology*. It should be said in his defence that a professional code of ethics had not yet been established and that less need was felt to cite sources.

Such criticism of Cyriacus' work in the light of modern methods in no way taints his work as a scholar. He was the first to give a fundamental role to material remains in the work of reconstructing a civilization and he had a sense of their historical importance. It took several centuries for this obvious fact to become generally accepted.

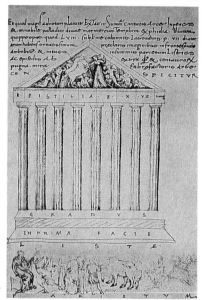

Cyriacus the visionary: a man before his time

At the end of his life, Cyriacus was aware that he was witnessing the death throes of the ancient world, which were linked to the advance of the Ottomans. That was why he rushed to gather as many remains as possible while Greece was still open to him. Humanists of his time were surprised and sometimes amused to see him nurture fantasies like the resurrection of antiquity. The historian Poggio writes, not without malice: 'Cyriacus of Ancona, a verbose and

ΕΡΜΗС · MERCVRIVS ·

inexhaustible speaker, sometimes deplored the fall and breakup of the Roman empire before our eyes; it seemed to cause him terrible anguish.'

Cyriacus did not have a clear grasp of the reality of the situation, and he probably did feel that it was his mission to attempt a rescue. In a church where he was deciphering epitaphs, he replied to a priest who had asked him what he was doing: 'It is my profession to resuscitate the dead of Hades. I have learned this art from the Pythia, the oracle of Apollo.'

Paganism and Christianity blend naturally in Cyriacus' expressions of his religious feelings. A sincere Catholic, he defended Christians' right to read pagan authors; he compared Christ to Jupiter and invoked the inspiration of Mercury (Hermes, the god of merchants), a relief of whom he drew at Delos. When leaving that island on a stormy night, he addressed the following prayer to him: 'Mercury, benevolent father of the arts, of the mind, of intelligence and of eloquence, who rekindled our soul and our courage by your most holy divinity, you who have watched over our joyful journey across Latium, Illyria, Greece, Asia and Egypt, over land and sea, continue, O noble genius, to protect our intelligence, our mind and our eloquence!'

In this drawing of the west facade of the Parthenon by Cyriacus (opposite, above), none of the proportions has been correctly drawn, though the artist did retain the exact number of columns and the representation of the Doric order. The metopes (below the frieze) have disappeared and the platform has been reduced to two steps. One notices the same fanciful approach in the reconstruction of the frieze, which depicts the dispute that took place in Attica between Poseidon and Athena. Athena is present in the centre, her long robe more reminiscent of the Renaissance than of antiquity. But Cyriacus has left out Poseidon and his team and has adorned the pediment with small nude and winged figures, none of whom bears any resemblance to the actual frieze.

Two drawings by Cyriacus of Ancona: a bust of Aristotle (opposite, below) and an archaic Hermes from Delos (left). His Latin name, Mercury, is written beside his Greek name, Hermes.

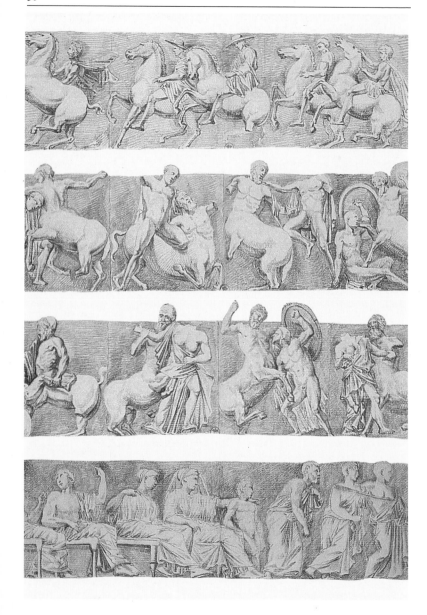

"When travelling in Greece, one should have Pausanias in one's hand in order to find the remarkable things that he found when he made this journey long ago and with the same curiosity. Take in the view of Tempe in Thessaly, of Parnassus, of the temple at Delphi and of the ruins of Athens. Bring back as many inscriptions as possible."

Jean-Baptiste Colbert, c. 1679

CHAPTER 3

LORDS AND SCHOLARS

Drawing of the metopes and frieze of the Parthenon (opposite), attributed to Jacques Carrey (1674). These images form a unique source of documentation, since so many of the statues and bas-reliefs have been seriously damaged or have disappeared. Left: a Greek head drawn by Jacob Spon.

The siege of Lemnos (left) illustrates the phenomenal advance of the Ottomans in the 15th century. After Attica (1456) and the Morea (1460), Euboea (1470) and then Lemnos (1478) werea captured.

Long before Constantinople fell to them in 1453, the Turks had begun their conquest of Greek territories. It took them only a few more years to annex the whole of continental Greece. In the 16th century they took Rhodes, Cyprus and the Cyclades; by the 17th century, only Crete was still resisting. The Venetians strove in vain to oppose this expansion, but there was no sequel to their victory at Lepanto in 1571. Constant hostilities, the fear of reprisal and distrust of the Turks, who were eager to accuse any inquisitive person of spying – not to mention the risks from piracy – reduced the number of travellers.

Travelling humanists

And yet a variety of new political circumstances was to make the Levant more accessible to Westerners. The establishment of Catholic (notably Jesuit and Capuchin) missions favoured contacts with Greek lands. While Greece was not itself the goal of travel in the 16th century, it was on the way to Jerusalem and Constantinople. Many pilgrims, merchants and, later, members of diplomatic missions could thus always be found there. These travellers shared a desire to see new things and an interest in ancient history and geography (Ptolemy's work was widely published). They were participating in the current of humanist thought that was developing outside Italy and that was greatly reinforced by Byzantine intellectuals who had emigrated to Western Europe.

Some of these travellers were scholars, like the naturalist and physician Pierre Belon (1517–64), who set off in 1546 to study the plants, animals and minerals of the Greek archipelago and to check the accuracy of the information that had been given by the naturalists and geographers of antiquity. But there were others whose apparent interest in the culture of antiquity concealed opinions and superstitions that they had inherited from the Middle Ages. Thus, André Thevet, the monk and geographer, stopped at a few islands on his return from a pilgrimage to the Holy Land. His account was typically weak and dull. It did nothing to dispel the general ignorance about the state of Greece – about the interior of the country and even about Athens. That was what led Martin Kraus, the famous Hellenist from Tübingen, Germany, to correspond with Greeks from Constantinople and to ask them whether Athens had been destroyed and replaced by a fishing village. Theodore Zigomalas' reply of 1554 proves that there was still an inhabited city, which was still adorned with its monuments, but it provides few other details.

These three drawings are the work of Nicolas de Nicolay, Henry II of France's first valet and geographer, who was a member of the retinue of the nobleman d'Aramont, the French ambassador to the Court of the Grand Turk. He travelled through Greece in 1551 and collected a large number of documents on the country, its inhabitants, their customs and their costumes. The vivid sketches with which he enlivened his descriptions ensured the success of his account (opposite, below: *Greek Nobleman;* left: *Lady of Chios;* below: *Greek Merchant*).

The passion for collecting

The era of great travels to Greece did not begin until the 17th century. But the taste for collecting, the desire to possess rare or precious objects, had burgeoned in the early 16th century. An interesting collection was a mark of prestige for nobles or for wealthy scholars. The collecting spirit also signalled an interest in the relics of the past as scholarly evidence. There were outstanding collections of antiquities in Italy from the 16th century.

At the beginning of the 17th century, Thomas Howard, the earl of Arundel, became one of the first large-scale collectors of art in England. His example was followed by King Charles I (who reigned from 1625 to 1649) and by Charles' favourite, the duke of

In 1568 Titian painted this portrait of Jacopo Strada, who is referred to as a Roman citizen and antiquarian. Like the collectors of his time, Strada was interested in medals, coins and statues. (He is holding a Venus.) Whenever he could, he sold his finds to the courts of Bavaria and Austria.

Buckingham. A diplomat who was passionately interested in art, Arundel decided to travel to Greece in search of sculptures and inscriptions. It has been said of him that he wanted to 'transplant ancient Greece to England'; to this end, he employed a network of agents who actively sought out antiquities for him, and he transformed his house and gardens into a museum to display his acquisitions.

An ambassador's odyssey

France was not left behind; Cardinal Mazarin, the 17th-century French statesman, Louis XIV

(who reigned France from 1643 to 1715) and Jean-Baptiste Colbert, his minister, had the idea of using French ambassadors in Constantinople to augment their collections and their libraries. Among these ambassadors, the Marquis de Nointel stands out clearly: a connoisseur of antiquities, endowed with a great mind and insatiable curiosity, Nointel spent the best part of his time as ambassador, from 1670 to 1679, travelling. His expedition to the Levant, in the course of which he spent a long time in the Cyclades in the company of the scholar Antoine Galland, who later became the first to translate the *Thousand and One Nights* into a European language, was a comprehensive exploration of all the areas he visited. The marquis had made a point of giving the journey a scholarly dimension by asking the consuls and missionaries staying in Greece to submit reports on the past and present state of the country. Unfortunately, Nointel combined scholarship with the greed of a treasure hunter. Wherever he went, he collected stelae, bas-reliefs and epigraphic texts.

On 4 November 1674 Nointel entered Athens with his customary pomp and ceremony. Granted permission to

At the time of the Marquis de Nointel's visit in 1674, the west pediment of the Parthenon was still almost intact. The overall composition of this frieze is known only through the drawing by Jacques Carrey, of which this is a detail. After the siege of 1687 Francesco Morosini, who wanted to carry a trophy back to Venice, ordered the removal of the group representing the horses and Athena's chariot. The sculptures fell accidentally and were shattered.

visit the Acropolis (a rare privilege at that time of armed peace between Venice and the Ottoman empire), he was overwhelmed by the splendour of the buildings and their decoration, which he was the first visitor to consider superior to that of Rome: 'Nobody has had as many opportunities as I have had to examine closely all those artistic riches, and one may say of those that can be seen in the castle around the Temple of Minerva [Athena] that they outshine the finest reliefs and statues of Rome....The most exalted comment that may be made about these originals is that they deserve to be placed in His Majesty's chambers or galleries, where they would enjoy the protection that the great monarch gives to the arts and to the sciences that produced them.'

The marquis may be forgiven for his sacrilegious intentions, which were shared by others, in view of the vitally important work he commissioned and which bears his name: the drawings of two hundred figures from the pediments, metopes and friezes of the Parthenon, parts of which shortly afterwards disappeared forever as a result of the bombardment of 1687.

Scholars and missionaries

In the last third of the 17th century, a whole movement of research was set in place, in which the role of the French was to be preeminent. Apart from the drawings of the Parthenon, the great documentary works produced include the Capuchins' Map of Athens (1670) and the reports by Father Babin (1672) and Consul Giraud (1675). These reports and the map were not the work of travellers but of people living in Athens who had acquired a deep knowledge of the country. They were all learned men who did not stand to benefit materially from the work they did. Consul Giraud, a highly cultivated man who spoke Greek and Turkish, was the enlightened cicerone of all travellers. According to Jacob Spon, for whom Giraud acted as a guide to the city, nobody was better informed about the antiquities of Athens; it was he who first attributed the sculptures of the Parthenon to Phidias.

In the 17th century the Acropolis was a fortress defended by a complex system of fortifications that reinforced the natural escarpment of the rock. A lower wall enclosed the Odeion of Herodes Atticus; above it, the second line of defence followed the ancient walls. From these crenellated ramparts emerge, on the left, the Propylaia – which had been walled since the Middle Ages – and the Frankish tower.

The French missionaries sent to Greece had received a sound intellectual training and exerted a very favourable influence on the safeguarding and study of the monuments. For example, the Capuchins acquired the Choregic Monument of Lysicrates, then commonly known as the Lantern of Demosthenes, which was later so often reproduced. These priests took advantage of their position to draw up the first general map of the city – the most detailed and most accurate one available at the time – since foreigners were treated as suspects by the Turks and were forbidden to draw or to write reports.

Shortly afterwards an account was published by a Jesuit missionary in Greece, Father Babin. The description Babin gave of Athens coincided quite precisely with the Capuchins' map. It seemed so complete and serious to the scholar Jacob Spon that he published it himself. With Pausanias in one hand and Father Babin's little book in the other, Spon visited Pericles' city himself a few years later.

The terrace of the Acropolis was covered with houses in which the garrison was lodged. The Parthenon stands out above these buildings. The roof and east pediment are not shown here, but the edifice was complete. A minaret rises from the southwest corner, indicating the presence of the mosque that had been there since 1460. The drawing shows the Acropolis in 1687, the year of the catastrophe.

Archaeology according to Jacob Spon

Spon occupies a special place among the scholars who
contributed to the birth of archaeology, a term he was the
first to use (in the preface to his work on epigraphy, the
Miscellanae eruditae antiquitatis). He believed that the
contributions of classical philology were no longer
sufficient to ensure the advancement of history; he saw a
need to go to other sources, to the ancient remains that
were 'books whose stone and marble pages have been
written on with iron points and chisels.' The systematic
use of inscriptions, the constant comparing of texts and
observable data – these were the rules of Spon's critical
method. He used it during the journey he made (without
an official commission) to satisfy his appetite for
antiquities. It took him into Greece via Italy and Asia
Minor in the company of an English botanist named
George Wheler.

Spon has left us only brief accounts of his crossing of
these regions, so preoccupied was he with discovering
and copying inscriptions wherever he went – Delos,
Delphi, Smyrna....

In the course of his
journey, Jacob Spon
copied more than two
thousand Greek and
Latin inscriptions. He is
seen here at Ephesos
immersed in his work of
deciphering inscriptions.
But archaeology is not
limited to the study of
coins and inscriptions.
'It is also', he said, 'by
means of objects that the
ancients transmitted
religion, history, politics,
arts and sciences.'

1676: Spon's stay in Athens

Accompanied by Wheler, Spon led the first great
archaeological exploration of Athens. The 17th-century
city was not the same as the one that Pausanias had seen.
Houses, Byzantine churches and mosques, as well as
ruins, covered the terrain. On the Acropolis, soldiers
lived in dilapidated houses that were scattered among the
monuments. Given these circumstances, the work of
investigation was almost impossible to carry out, and the
surveillance of the garrison and the hostility of the
inhabitants made it even harder. Nevertheless, the
monuments were then more numerous and better
preserved than they are today. They had not suffered too
much from the presence of the Ottomans. Noble
memories associated with the city's history undoubtedly
helped to protect it in the eyes of the authorities, and
all were forbidden to touch the sculptures of the 'temple
of the idols', which was how the Muslims referred to
the Parthenon.

In the course of his trip, Spon attempted to restore
name and origin to places and monuments by comparing

Guided by Consul
Giraud, Spon and
George Wheler discover
Athens. Going beyond
legends and traditions,
Spon said, 'reconciles
monuments with
history....The surest
approach in these matters
is not a to accept any
prejudice from generally
accepted opinions if one
does not examine them
oneself and if one does
not weigh them against
the balance of reason.'

Spon started to collect and draw coins in Lyons when he was still a very young man. He also sold them, since as an 'antiquarian physician' he had modest financial resources. He paid for the publication of the first volume of the *Miscellanae* himself; the second one never appeared. A tolerant humanist and determined Protestant, Spon went into exile in Switzerland as a result of the revocation of the Edict of Nantes in 1685 and later died there.

his own observations with the accounts of ancient authors and the few descriptions of contemporary travellers. He did indeed manage to correct a large number of generally accepted mistakes. He was the first person to identify the Temple of Athena Nike, demolished in 1687 to make room for a rampart (and later reconstructed); he interpreted the Choregic Monument of Lysicrates correctly ('a monument of glory, erected in honour of those who had triumphed in one of those famous actions [a contest of music and dance]'). He also recognized that the Tower of the Winds, usually referred to as the Tomb of Socrates, was actually a hydraulic clock.

But Spon also made mistakes. He assumed that the caryatids were the Graces of Socrates, which Pausanias had seen below the Propylaia. He speaks of his admiration of the Parthenon: 'The sight of it imposed a certain respect, and we stood there looking at it for a considerably long time.' Yet it was precisely there that he made his most serious errors. He confused the pediments, not realizing that the temple's openings were to the east. He rejected the attribution of the sculptures to Phidias and dated them to the time of Hadrian, since he thought he recognized the figures. ('The last two statues on that side are those of the Emperor Hadrian,' he wrote, 'seated and half-naked and, beside him, his wife Sabina. I do not think that this noteworthy fact has been noticed before.') This was an unfortunate mistake,

The Tower of the Winds was a popular monument in Athens as early as the 17th century. This octagonal tower (drawn by Spon), made of white marble and decorated with figures symbolizing the winds, contained a hydraulic clock. It was built in the 1st century BC.

but it was quickly accepted and was still current in the 19th century. In spite of such errors, Spon's narrative was a landmark. The public recognized it as such, and it became immensely popular: *The Journey to Italy, Dalmatia, Greece and the Levant*, which was translated into several languages, was to remain the guide of informed travellers until the early 19th century.

An unexpected misfortune was to add to the work's fame: Spon was one of the last Europeans to have seen and described the Parthenon while it was still intact. On 26 September 1687, during the siege of Athens by the Venetians, a bomb fell on the temple, reducing it to ruins. The Turks had been storing their munitions there.

'We shall always deplore the fact that a monument built with a perfection that enabled it to defy the rigours of time and the barbarity of men for two thousand years has been destroyed by Christian Europe.' This condemnation of the Italians' wrongdoings by the Comte de Laborde might just as easily be applied to the French, the British or the Germans. All these 'civilized' Europeans later took the Parthenon apart and shipped the sculpted treasures of classical Greece to their countries without remorse.

This drawing by the Venetian engineer Giacomo Verneda shows the bombardment of the Acropolis, which he witnessed. An enormous explosion followed by a fire ravaged the Parthenon. The roof was destroyed, the wall of the cella and many of the columns collapsed, leaving the temple cut in two, and part of Phidias' frieze was shattered. The explosion was so powerful that debris from the building was projected into the camp of the besieging army.

"When I left Paris in order to visit Greece, I simply wanted to satisfy the passion I felt in my youth for the most famous lands of antiquity. I could taste in advance the pleasure of crossing this famous and beautiful region with Homer and Herodotus in my hands. At last I was promising myself a state of permanent intoxication in a land where the smallest rock appears to the imagination to be inhabited by gods and heroes."

Comte de Choiseul-Gouffier, 1782

CHAPTER 4

THE GREEK MYTH

The journey undertaken by the painter James Stuart and the architect Nicholas Revett and their illustrated work mark a decisive stage in our knowledge of the monuments of Athens. Opposite: a self-portrait by Stuart, *The Athenian,* drawing the Erechtheion.

In the 18th century Greece was in fashion. Travellers went there in large numbers – both the traditional travellers and an influx of artists and of young people from wealthy backgrounds who had completed their studies and were making the Grand Tour around the Mediterranean. Nearly all took up their pens upon their return, and the published accounts were increasingly well illustrated and generally very successful.

This craze was in keeping with the spirit of the century. The philosophy of the Enlightenment – the promotion of nature and reason – had, of course, been central to the value system of antiquity. So, after the mid-18th century, we find a return to the aesthetic and moral values of the ancient world. Greece, 'home of the arts' and 'educator of taste',

This cave, near Vari, on the slopes of Mt Hymettos, was decorated by a certain Archidamos, who said that he had been inspired by the nymphs. Richard Chandler and William Pars (who painted this watercolour) were captivated by its blend of anatural beauty and archaeological artifacts – typical of the sensibility of the time.

became the school at which Europe came to study.

In a different domain, Greece stepped out from the shade and made its appearance on the political scene. The weakening of the Ottoman empire, which had been undermined by internal anarchy, left the road open for the ambitions of the great powers, who contemplated its dismemberment and the liberation of the Greeks. In a desire to expand southwards, Russia took a stand as the protector of the Orthodox people and fomented uprisings. The Russo-Turkish wars of the 18th century further accelerated the decline of the Ottoman empire.

Easier travel

This situation provoked a change in the Turkish attitude towards foreigners. Supervision became more relaxed, and visitors could explore the country more easily, touring the interior as far as Macedonia, Thessaly or Maina. At the same time the export of antiquities surged, and the Turkish authorities closed their eyes. It was true that all journeys still involved their own dangers; in order to protect themselves from groups of *klephtes* (brigands), travellers had to be accompanied by janissaries from the elite corps of Turkish troops. The plague was often rampant, too, but the era of perilous voyages of exploration was coming to an end, while the era of romantic travel was just beginning.

For their part, the Greeks sought to benefit from this new state of affairs. With Russian protection, they increased their maritime and commercial power. With the improvement in the economy, a middle class was created and a national feeling developed, drawing much inspiration from the ideas of the Enlightenment and from the pedagogical efforts made by Greeks of the diaspora. Thus, Adamantios Koraïs, a Greek who lived in Paris from 1788 until his death in 1833, promoted ancient Greek authors and gave a fixed form to the modern Greek language by compiling the first modern Greek dictionary. Foreign travellers also played a part in the awakening of the consciousness of their identity within the Greek people. By virtue of the awe in which they held antiquity, foreign visitors reawoke the ancestral memory of a subject people.

The funerary monument of Philopappos was erected by the Athenians in the early 2nd century AD in honour of a Syrian prince who was the city's benefactor. It stands alone on the summit of the Mouseion. With its curved facade turned towards the Acropolis and decorated with pilasters and statues, it has long been a source of inspiration to artists. This watercolour by James Stuart is a very faithful rendition.

Until the end of the 18th century, travellers, who most often visited Greece on the way to the Middle East, discovered the Greek ruins of Asia Minor. In 1765–6, the Hellenist Richard Chandler and the painter William Pars visited the sanctuary of the oracle of Apollo at Didyma, near Miletos. Here, Pars faithfully reproduces a capital of the temple but puts it into an exotic setting. This mixture of archaeological accuracy and a taste for the picturesque is one of the features of the travel accounts produced before the 19th century. Alexander Kinglake's *Eothen* is an example of this genre. Meanwhile, a British colonel, William Leake (1777–1860), who was also an antiquarian, defined rules for the writing of scholarly accounts. He was the founder of historical geography.

French scholars and philologists on assignment

Not everything changed in the 18th century. Official expeditions continued to be sent out. Joseph Pitton de Tournefort, one of the famous botanists of the time, left in 1700 for the Greek islands 'to check, on the spot, what exactly the ancients knew concerning natural history, especially plants.' He did not neglect the antiquities, however, which he described with a critical spirit. Most of the other expeditions went with the aim of discovering ancient coins and manuscripts for the royal library, such as Father Fourmont's mid-18th-century expedition, which still arouses controversy today. Fourmont boasted that he had destroyed Sparta. He brought back a mass of inscriptions, some of which were fake. At the end of the century, the great Enlightenment Hellenist Jean-Baptiste d'Ansse de Villoison continued this untiring and extremely disappointing search for manuscripts. He did bring back a number of ancient inscriptions, but philology was no longer considered all that fascinating.

French botanist Joseph Pitton de Tournefort made one of the last great scientific journeys that did not have literary aspirations. Above: a female statue from Kéa, perhaps representing Nemesis. The drawing is by Aubriet, who accompanied Tournefort.

Inner door of the cella of the Temple of Apollo on Naxos (6th century BC). 'This door, consisting of only three pieces of white marble, is of a simplicity which is very appealing; two pieces form the uprights and the third the lintel.' This precise, if dry, description, which is quite typical of Tournefort's style, is illustrated by a watercolour by Thomas Hope (c. 1795).

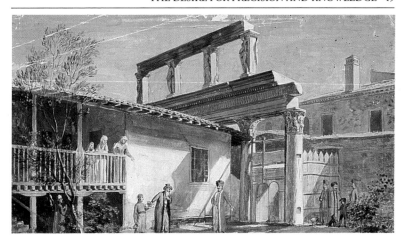

The intervention of English architects

Architects seeking new stylistic models opened the way to the study of archaeology. The impetus came from Italy. The discovery of Herculaneum in 1738 and Pompeii in 1748 and the excavations there renewed people's understanding of antiquity. Scholars and artists found themselves in direct contact with a civilization that had been profoundly influenced by classical and Hellenistic Greece; in Italy they found copies of Greek sculpture and frescoes that had been inspired by Greek paintings.

At the same time, the exploration of the temples of Paestum (southern Italy) and Sicily revealed the Doric order, which, because of its massive proportions, architects at first found disconcerting and primitive.

It was at that moment that the field of research was extended to Greece itself. The first to set off were two Britons, a painter, James Stuart, and an architect, Nicholas Revett, who had met in Rome. Both were interested in archaeology and devised a plan to identify, measure and draw the antiquities of Athens. The Society of Dilettanti of London subsidized their venture and commissioned them to assemble models of ornamentation destined to be used by British architects.

The Society was originally an elite social club, which had been founded in 1733 by the Earl of Sandwich.

This Corinthian portico surmounted by a row of pillars that are decorated with mythological figures in relief (2nd century AD) was situated in the Spanish-Jewish quarter of Thessalonica. In this painting, James Stuart and Nicholas Revett are received by a rabbi. The ruins were dismantled and transported to the Louvre in 1865.

Stuart and Revett in Athens

Previous pages: the 'Theseion', the best-preserved of the temples of Athens (5th century BC), stood slightly to one side of the city, bordered by cultivated fields, when James Stuart painted it in 1751. Although it was actually dedicated to Hephaestos, the temple owes its traditional name to the figurative depiction of Theseus' exploits on the friezes. Transformed into a church, it suffered little damage under the Turks. In the foreground, a scene from everyday life: Albanian agricultural workers winnow corn, supervised by a Turkish foreman.

Left: the Arch of Hadrian, a monumental marble gateway, marked the border between the ancient city and the Roman city, or New Athens. Today, it still looks basically as James Stuart has shown it, with its two-storeyed facade, the lower arcade supporting the Corinthian portico with its three bays.

The society's initial aim was to support the arts, but it became more serious and brought together the greatest connoisseurs of ancient art. It therefore exerted considerable influence on English taste, commissioned expeditions and financed the publication of their findings – those of Stuart and Revett in Greece and those of Revett and the British Hellenist Richard Chandler in Asia Minor.

From 1751 to 1753 Stuart and Revett stayed in Athens, later visiting the islands, where they also produced reports. They were remarkably active. They drew up a plan of the Acropolis, delineating the buildings with precision, writing a scholarly analysis of them and even excavating in order to verify their theories – as when they examined the foundations of the Tower of the Winds.

They did make some errors. Believing that they were rectifying an error made by Spon, they placed the Temple of Athena Nike back into the southern wing of the Propylaia; at the Parthenon, they did not notice the inclination of the columns or the curve of the pavement. But on the whole their writing was authoritative and it was published in a magnificent work that included engraved plates and maps. The first volume appeared in 1762, and Ennio Visconti, the great Italian archaeologist, later wrote: 'Stuart was the first person in Europe to reveal the true style of Greek architecture.'

The picturesque ruins of Julien David Le Roy

The publication of the second volume was delayed, and Stuart and Revett found themselves forestalled by Julien David Le Roy, an architect in Rome. He made a study trip to Greece at the same time as the two British scholars.

A very proud man, he hurried to publish his *Ruins of the Finest Monuments of Greece* in 1758 in advance of his rivals. This was the first time that the Hellenic buildings were reproduced and the first time that the Greek Doric order and its evolution were studied in their true proportions. Had it not previously been maintained that the architecture of the Parthenon did not match the quality of its sculpture? Le Roy also revealed the Ionic

"The ideas that ruins awaken in me are great," said French encyclopaedist Denis Diderot. This view is expressed in the drawings of Julien David Le Roy: he invokes the freedom of inspiration and the right to alter proportions and perspectives.

order of the Erechtheion. As a professor at the Academy of Architecture in Paris, he worked hard to have Greek models adopted there.

But Le Roy's drawings lack precision and bear the marks of fantasy. He was evidently influenced by the taste for representing ruins that was so characteristic of the 18th-century sensibility, and which prints by the Italian architect Giambattista Piranesi helped to spread. Eager, above all, to create a romantic impression, artists of the period were seldom faithful to the reality of the Greek landscape or ancient sites. Symbolizing the passage of time, the disappearance of civilization and the durability of nature, ruins – whether the main subject or merely a decorative element in a picture – always

These two Ionic columns supporting an entablature (below) are the remains of Hadrian's aqueduct on Lykabettos Hill. They were destroyed in 1778.

provided an atmosphere of meditation and dreaming.

The final great publication of the century was *Picturesque Voyage* by the Comte de Choiseul-Gouffier, who was later to be the French ambassador to Constantinople. Like his predecessor, the Marquis de Nointel, whom he resembled in many respects, Choiseul-Gouffier put together a team of scholars and artists. His account, which has no archaeological pretensions but which is extremely well informed, reflects a radiant image of Greece in keeping with the myth that was fostered by contemporary education, marking an entire generation.

The Greece of dreams

And yet, no work aroused as much public interest as the *Voyage of the Young Anacharsis*, published in 1788 by Father Jean-Jacques Barthélemy. This book, part history, part novel, told of the travels of a Scythian through ancient Greece. It was immensely popular throughout Europe, and it was one of the first works to be translated into modern Greek. Through tableaux of domestic life and the Panathenaia (a festival celebrating Athena), it depicted Greece as an elegant, refined, pleasant land, as befitted the European taste of the day. Modern values and attitudes were blended with those of the ancients.

Panoramic view of Athens by Louis François Cassas (1784). In the centre are the two groups of imposing columns of the Temple of Olympian Zeus, between which appear the outline of the Acropolis and, on its slopes, the Albanian quarter. On the left stand the arches of the Odeion of Herodes Atticusa, the 'Theseion' and the Monument of Philopappos.

The author was not uninformed, however. He was an expert on ancient languages, knew the civilization and was familiar with classical authors. But he had not been to Greece, he had no instinctive sympathy with the Greeks and, 18th-century gentleman that he was, he gives a conventional and false image, justifying the novelist Stendhal's verdict: 'The country in the world in which the Greeks are least well known is France, and that is because of the Abbé Barthélemy's book.'

The great publications, the *Voyage of the Young Anacharsis* and the increased knowledge of everyday life in Herculaneum and Pompeii and of Etruscan artifacts and tombs (which contained many Greek vases) all contributed to the popularity of Greece and the obsession with antiquity at the end of the 18th century.

Greek renaissance

The 'Greek' style was not merely a fad; it reflected as well a need for renewal in literature, art and social conventions as a reaction against the decline of the Baroque age. The neo-classical revolution was especially evident in architecture. In England it was heralded by the pavilion that James Stuart built in Hagley Park, a reconstruction of the Doric temple known as the

A composition in the antique style, in which Hubert Robert, known for his paintings of ruins, has artificially brought together elements of architecture and sculpture: a column, a broken bas-relief, a statue of Athena and fragments of capitals. Female figures enliven the scene. In the foreground, two women are drawing. These fake picturesque ruins and elegiac evocations characterized the pre-Romantic sensibility and its obsession with antiquity.

Theseion; Nicholas Revett built a portico in the Delian order at Standlynch in Wiltshire. In France the Doric order appeared in the crypt of Sainte-Geneviève, designed by Jacques-Germain Soufflot (the Panthéon) and in the portico of the Convent of La Charité, the work of Jacques-Denis Antoine, a pupil of Le Roy.

New views of art

Architects were not the only people to contribute to the formation of modern archaeology. The Comte de Caylus and Johann Joachim Winckelmann directed research on antiquities towards the study of art. Both were enamoured of Greece, though neither managed to visit it.

The Comte de Caylus played a central role as an archaeologist. Breaking with philological tradition, which insisted that written evidence was the only sound source for the reconstruction of the past, Caylus proposed 'looking at monuments as the proof and expression of a style that reigned in a given century and country.' He applied his method in his *Collection of Egyptian, Etruscan, Greek, Roman and Gallic Antiquities* (1752–67). Because of his interest in techniques, tools and materials,

Set in the study of a person with an interest in antiquities, an ape in a dressing gown examines a coin with a magnifying glass. Here, the 18th-century French painter Jean-Baptiste-Siméon Chardin is supposed to be ridiculing the leading antiquarian of the day, the Comte de Caylus. The painter has dramatized the philosophers' opinion of antiquarians as pedants and lunatics who were said to study 'rusty saucepans and broken vases'.

which were of greater importance to him than aesthetic appreciation, Caylus' work seems distinctly modern. At the same time, Winckelmann, a German, 'invented' the history of Greek art. He enjoyed astonishing prestige in his own lifetime and for centuries afterwards. He was a revolutionary even in his first book, *Reflections on the Imitation of Greek Works in Painting and in Sculpture* (1755). At a time when Greco-Latin antiquity was perceived as a whole, he intuited that there was a Greek civilization that had not been altered by the Roman tradition: 'The eminent general characteristic of the Greek masterpieces is a noble simplicity and a silent grandeur,' he said. Winckelmann based his aesthetic theory on the search for the ideal of beauty, which he identified with the *Apollo Belvedere*, the *Laocoön*, and the Medici *Venus,* and which he proposed that artists should imitate: 'The only means we have of being great, or even inimitable, if that is possible, is to imitate the ancients.'

In his *History of Art*, his magnum opus, Winckelmann formulated the idea of the evolution of art, 'which is born, flourishes and declines with the civilizations in the midst of which it develops.' He attempted to devise a classification of Greek art based upon the notion of style: the Antique or Archaic style; the Sublime or 'Grand, Elevated' style of Phidias; the Beautiful style of Praxiteles (4th century BC); and the Decadent (Imitative) style (1st century BC and Roman period). This classification contained errors that are clear to us today. Winckelmann based his history of Greek art on the study of Roman copies of Greek originals or on Hellenistic statues that he was unable to date, or which he took to be classical works, as in the case of the *Laocoön*.

Winckelmann was an archaeologist in the full sense of the term. He published collections of antiquities; he followed the excavation of Herculaneum and Pompeii very closely and was extremely critical of the methods of excavation; and he dreamed of excavating Olympia. He was one of the first people to formulate the idea of research in the sanctuaries of Greece, following Pausanias' example, a project that would not be undertaken until the 19th century.

Johann Joachim Winckelmann (1717–68) was considered as fascinating as his works. He came from a very modest background, had a difficult youth, studied theology, which he hated, and took lowly jobs. None of this dampened his intellectual enthusiasm or shook his belief in art. His success in Rome, where he was attached to the pontifical court, his life surrounded by works of art, his growing fame and, finally, his murder in Trieste made him legendary.

"But who, of all the plunderers of
  yon fane
On high, where Pallas linger'd, loth
  to flee
The latest relic of her ancient reign;
The last, the worst, dull spoiler, who
  was he?
Blush, Caledonia! such thy son could
  be!"

Lord Byron, 1812

CHAPTER 5
THE PERIOD OF THE GREAT PLUNDERERS

The *Dying Warrior* (left), part of a temple pediment from Aegina, and the *Venus de Milo* (opposite) were bought by Bavaria and France respectively.

In the two decades that preceded the liberation of Greece, a series of scandals broke out relating to the plundering of antiquities on an international scale. Ironically, they brought about a profound transformation in the understanding of Greek sculpture. The advantage scholars gained from this does not justify the manner in which the pediments of the Parthenon or the temple of Aegina, the frieze of Bassae or the *Venus de Milo* found their way into European museums, even when looked at from the point of view of the time.

Not content with pillaging Greece, the great powers of the day also plundered each others' collections. Archaeology was part of war or served as an alibi for

This fresco of 1848 by Wilhelm von Kaulbach is a celebration of Ludwig I of Bavaria in his role as collector. The king stands out against the facade of the Glyptothek, looking at a group of antique sculptures. Winckelmann rests his hand on the statue of Apollo holding a lyre.

it. A scientific expedition was thus added to Napoleon's Egyptian campaign; the only profits gained by the French from that war were the discovery of the Rosetta Stone in 1799, the deciphering of hieroglyphics and the birth of Egyptology.

The founding of the great European museums

At the end of the 18th century and the beginning of the 19th, the hunt for art treasures was intensified by the needs of great public museums that were springing up all

To the left, behind Winckelmann, are three famous antiquities that had recently joined the king's collection: a warrior from Aegina, the *Barberini Faun* and a Pallas Velletri. To the king's left, in the foreground, Haller von Hallerstein is holding the vase. (The latter led excavations in Athens on Ludwig's behalf.)

over Europe: the Pio-Clementino Museum in the Vatican, whose earliest catalogue dates from 1792; the British Museum in London, founded in 1753; the Musée Napoléon in Paris in 1801; and the Glyptothek in Munich in 1830. These museums were hungry for fine pieces whose prestige would contribute to the glory of the state that owned them.

Thus, Napoleon did not hesitate to plunder the Italian collections. In 1797, by victor's right, he requisitioned all the great landmarks of Greek sculpture upon which Winckelmann had based his history of art, including the *Laocoön* and the *Wounded Gaul*. These statues were exhibited in the Louvre until 1816, clearly showing that Paris had become the new Rome *and* the new Athens. If Napoleon had not returned from Elba and been defeated at Waterloo, the statues might have remained there to this day!

The *Laocoön* arriving at the Louvre (below). The transfer of works of art aroused a wide-ranging debate in 1796. Whereas the French archaeologist Quatremère de Quincy compared Napoleon to Verres, the Roman politician notorious for pillage, others supported the export of art: 'It is time for all the monuments of the Greeks' genius to leave a land that is no longer worthy of possessing them. They were created in a free country: it is only in France that they may, today, find a homeland,' said one pundit.

The only scarcity in these collections was original works. The great powers, as well as the not-so-great, did all they could to acquire them. And the museums' hunger for originals is still an important force in the visible (and the invisible) antiquities market.

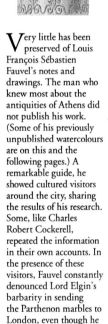

Political factors explain the transfer of antiquities from Greece: there was no political authority strong enough to prevent the pillaging. The Ottoman empire was being worn down by incessant wars with Russia, France and Britain, and the sultan of Turkey could not refuse his protector of the moment anything. From 1799 to 1806 the protector was Great Britain. In Greece itself, it was not difficult to pay for and obtain permission from

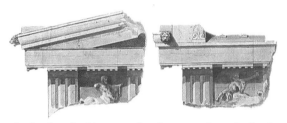

the local authorities to undertake excavations. As for the Greek communities, they had no means of opposing the removal of their heritage.

Greece had become an important centre, attracting tourists of every nationality, especially the British. This was in part because of the political situation: a rapprochement had taken place between the Turks and the British when Italy was closed to the latter because of the French conquest and the continental blockade.

Lord Elgin in the East

It was in these exceptional circumstances that Lord Thomas Elgin was sent as ambassador to Constantinople. According to some authorities, the British government was responsible for a simultaneous expedition to Greece, the aim of which was to acquire works of art and to prevent France from controlling the antiquities market. Others see this as Lord Elgin's personal project, excited as he was by the opportunity that presented itself to him 'of making his embassy profitable to the

Very little has been preserved of Louis François Sébastien Fauvel's notes and drawings. The man who knew most about the antiquities of Athens did not publish his work. (Some of his previously unpublished watercolours are on this and the following pages.) A remarkable guide, he showed cultured visitors around the city, sharing the results of his research. Some, like Charles Robert Cockerell, repeated the information in their own accounts. In the presence of these visitors, Fauvel constantly denounced Lord Elgin's barbarity in sending the Parthenon marbles to London, even though he himself had taken some valuable pieces.

progress of the fine arts in Great Britain.' In any case, Franco-British antagonism certainly played a role in the sacking of the monuments of Athens.

It was obvious to any observer that, at the beginning of the 19th century, the marbles of the Acropolis were destined to leave, either for London or for Paris. In 1784 the Comte de Choiseul-Gouffier, the French ambassador

B ased in Athens from 1803 as the French consul, Fauvel lived in this house on the ancient Agora. In this picture (left), he is shown painting, surrounded by antiquities (on the right, a metope from the Parthenon). His collection was dispersed at the time of the Greek War of Independence.

A bove: one of Fauvel's watercolours.

to the Ottoman empire, had installed one of his agents in Athens. After the French Revolution caused Choiseul-Gouffier to be exiled, his agent, who remained faithful to the monarchy, stayed on in Greece, formed his own museum and controlled the antiquities market, preventing travellers from buying artifacts. But in August 1798 the agent was imprisoned, with all other French people living in Greece, and his possessions were sequestered. The ground was thus open to the projects of the British.

The Elgin Marbles

July 1801 marked the beginning of the pillaging of the Parthenon and, more generally, of the whole of the Acropolis. This was to continue until 1805, when the removal of works and excavation were prohibited. Teams of workers, under the direction of an Italian painter, Giovanni Battista Lusieri, who was Lord Elgin's authorized representative, seized the dozen or so statues remaining on the pediments or buried in the ruins and took down fifty-six slabs from the frieze, as well as fifteen of the metopes, the frieze of the Temple of Athena Nike and one of the caryatids from the Erechtheion – to cite only the most famous pieces.

In justification of his actions, Lord Elgin did have two arguments which should be given their due. One was that he had observed all the legal forms and had received permission from the authorities. The fact that these authorities were Turkish and therefore (it could be argued) did not have a moral right to sell the Parthenon sculpture was hardly his fault.

Fauvel's watercolour of the Lion Gate at Mycenae (above).

These two views of the Parthenon (left) reveal the scale of the destruction. The first, by the painter William Gell, dates from 1801; the second is by Lord Byron's companion, John Hobhouse, who lived in the temple in 1810. They confirm Edward Dodwell's account: 'I had the inexpressible displeasure of being present when the Parthenon was stripped of some of its finest sculptures and when some parts of its architecture were demolished. I saw several metopes at the southeast corner of the temple being detached.... to remove them, the superb cornice that covered them had to be knocked down.'

The Erechtheion,
which stands on the
Acropolis and was
finished in c. 394 BC,
brought together the
most ancient cults of the
city-state. Its complexity
is clear in this
watercolour by Edward
Dodwell. Shown are the
porch of the caryatids,
the central body enclosed
by Ionic half columns,
and part of the north
porch. The interior had
been entirely transformed
by the installation of
a church and then of a
harem, but the exterior
was in a reasonably good
state of preservation when
Lord Elgin's team
arrived. Giovanni Battista
Lusieri had the second
caryatid removed and
replaced in 1801 with a
brick pillar.

The other was that the sculptures were neglected and ignored and, without Elgin's intervention, would almost certainly have perished altogether.

Outrage in the face of the pillage

Well before the marbles left Greek soil, Lord Elgin's actions aroused a wave of condemnation, especially from foreigners who had witnessed the dismantling of the sculptures. Those who came later, such as the Vicomte de Chateaubriand (1768–1848), the French writer and statesman, found the Parthenon in a desolate state of ruin. He was among those who wrote deploring this devastation but who nevertheless did not hesitate to carry off valuable fragments himself.

Chateaubriand was not the worst of them. He admits in all innocence: 'When coming down from the citadel of the Acropolis I took a piece of marble from the Parthenon; I had also picked up a fragment of stone from Agamemnon's tomb; and since then, I have always taken something from the monuments I have visited. They are not such fine souvenirs of my travels as those carried off by Monsieur de Choiseul and Lord Elgin, but they are enough for me.' (*Itinerary from Paris to Jerusalem*, 1811).

The detractor who dealt a fatal blow to Elgin's reputation was Lord Byron, the English Romantic poet. In 1812, when Byron's *Childe Harold's Pilgrimage* and *The Curse of Minerva* appeared, Lord Elgin became 'the spoiler',

L ord Byron (left, in Eastern dress) discovered Greece in the course of his Grand Tour. He was outraged by Fauvel's practices and by the form of Hellenism he saw in the behaviour of foreign visitors to Greece.

'the sacrilegious man' who carried off 'the last poor plunder from a bleeding land'. The right of the powerful to strip the weak of their heritage came into question.

'They are Roman, my Lord'

The Elgin Marbles gave rise to another polemic in addition to Byron's. From the time of the marbles' arrival in London, all the artists, connoisseurs and art lovers rushed to see them. The effect they had on the artistic world was overwhelming: 'The Elgin Marbles are far superior to all the treasures of Italy,' wrote one viewer. Strangely, however, the Earl of Sandwich's group of antiquarians, the Dilettanti, did not share this enthusiasm. Their spokesman, Richard Payne Knight, an eminent aesthetician, delivered a verdict against which there could be no appeal: the marbles were inferior. Far

The arrival in England of the marbles of the Parthenon appealed to the imagination of artists of the time, as this imaginary presentation of the collection makes clear. The president of the Royal Academy of Arts wrote to Lord Elgin: 'By bringing these treasures to London.... you have founded a new Athens for the example and emulation of the English scholar.'

from coming from Phidias' studio, they were Roman and dated from Hadrian's time, as Spon had asserted earlier. Although this was erroneous, the Dilettanti were only voicing the taste of their time, as expressed by Winckelmann. The imitation of nature, the realism that bursts forth from Phidias' friezes, shocked them and challenged the idea they had formed of perfection.

This controversy began to jeopardize the plan by which the state was to buy the collections of Lord Elgin, who was in debt. In 1814, to restore the marbles' prestige, Elgin asked Ennio Quirino Visconti to evaluate them. This peerless connoisseur found them dazzling. He made every effort to refute all Knight's criticisms; the Italian sculptor Canova, who worked in Paris, and then Quatremère de Quincy (the 'French Winckelmann') shared Visconti's emotion. De Quincy wrote: 'Who has not seen the Elgin Marbles has not seen anything,' and, on the subject of the pediments: 'They show such truth that it frightens me.' These expert opinions determined the committee's decision, but the purchase price of £35,000 was a disappointment to Lord Elgin.

In August 1816, having become the property of the British nation, the sculptures were transported to the British Museum. From the time they were installed,

View of the room in the British Museum in which the Elgin Marbles were installed in 1819. One recognizes, on the right, the Dionysos from the east pediment of the Parthenon and, on the left, the Cephissos from the west pediment. Friezes and metopes were hung on the wall. Among the onlookers are the artists who were the first to pay homage to Phidias' genius.

drawings, plaster casts and engravings of them spread throughout Britain and abroad. Although it could not be said that they produced a transformation in the public's taste, as Lord Elgin had hoped, they did, at least, revolutionize the understanding of Greek art.

Distinguished seekers of antiquities discover Aegina and Bassae

On 22 April 1811 the last of the Parthenon marbles left Athens on a boat bound for Malta. Lord Byron and his

The signatures of the members of the Xeneion, an association of friends who shared an enthusiasm for Greece and things Greek (above).

agent were passengers on the same boat. At Piraeus that boat crossed the path of a light vessel that was taking four friends to Aegina: two were Englishmen, the architect Charles Robert Cockerell and John Foster, and two were Germans, Karl Haller von Hallerstein and Jacob Linck. In that same year, they discovered the pediments of Aegina and, with other companions, also excavated at Bassae, in Arcadia.

This was the first international association of archaeologists, which some have, no doubt wrongly, called an association of robbers of antiquities. In fact, the trade in antiquities was not the most important object of their activities; they all belonged to the circle of writers and artists who were passionately in love with Greece. Apart from the British, who did not join the group until it reached Athens, the 'inventors' of Aegina and of Bassae had become friends in Rome: Haller von Hallerstein, a hardworking German aristocrat and talented architect who had trained in Berlin, and Karl Friedrich Schinkel, a German architect and painter who was tormented by

A portrait of Charles Robert Cockerell by Haller von Hallerstein (far left) and (near left) a portrait of Haller by Otto Magnus von Stackelberg. P. O. Brönsted defined the friends' aims: 'We have joined together, Haller, Linck, Stackelberg and I, to draw and to write the history of the best things that we have seen, felt and learned in various regions of Greece, taking into special consideration the movements of art and history of Hellenic antiquity.'

an urgent need for aesthetic and moral perfection, two Danes, and a Baltic baron, Otto Magnus von Stackelberg. Von Stackelberg, an art lover who spoke at least ten languages, published the Temple of Bassae in 1826 with his own drawings.

In 1810 the Danes had dragged their friends to Greece. They must have had considerable courage to have survived a shipwreck, escaped from the British and avoided a Tunisian pirate. In Athens they met Foster and Cockerell, both of whom came from families of wealthy architects. They formed an association called the Xeneion, whose rules reveal the spirit that motivated them: the only qualification for membership was 'enthusiasm for Greece, ancient literature and the fine arts'. They asserted that 'random distinctions between nations are abolished'. Their intentions were generous, but their work eventually stimulated international competition, a force that dominated research in Greece throughout the 19th century and also for a large part of the 20th century.

Great Britain, France and Bavaria were

The amazement caused by the Bassae frieze depicting the Greeks fighting the Amazons (drawn below by Otto Magnus von Stackelberg) is well expressed by John Foster in a letter of 25 September 1812: 'Neither in Paris nor in Rome is there such an accomplished frieze, one that is so long and so beautiful. In many of its sections, the limbs of the human and animal figures and those of the centaurs are entirely in relief, set free from the background. These works, displaying such a raised technique, give the most extraordinary impression.'

This watercolour by John Foster shows the state of the Temple of Bassae at the time of the excavations, which the architect Haller von Hallerstein describes in lyrical terms: 'Every day, we had at work fifty, sixty or more men. To prevent the work from being too difficult and unappealing and to allow it to be carried out with joy and energy, they had to relax and have a break to the accompaniment of music. In the evening they danced with the beautiful shepherdesses of Arcady beneath the porticoes of the temple, which were gradually being revealed.'

prepared to take part in the auction that was held in Malta for the statues of Aegina, which the friends had discovered in April 1811. The German contingent was aided by the manoeuvres of one Gropius, a character who was himself the object of some competition. (He was the consul of Great Britain, of Prussia and of Austria in turn.) He was finally able to secure eighteen statues in good condition and numerous fragments for King Ludwig I of Bavaria for 100,000 gold francs – a relatively modest sum to have paid for Greek originals. The statues passed from Malta to Rome, in order to be restored in the studio of the Danish sculptor Bertel Thorvaldsen. The frieze of Bassae, uncovered in July 1812, was the object of a successful bid by Great Britain: it went to the British Museum for £19,000.

Head of Athena from the west pediment at Aegina (c. 500 BC).

Old and new mentalities

Several features of these spectacular ventures belong to a prescientific mentality and archaeology.

An excavation was conducted rather like a treasure hunt or an outing in the country. It would be too harsh to condemn the young men involved for having profited from a few idyllic moments when they were exposed daily to such assorted dangers as shipwrecks, looters, fevers and death – two of them died in Greece. Should they be reproached for having sold the antiquities they discovered? Archaeology had not yet lost the mercantile goals it had had since the Middle Ages. But it must be admitted that these genuine lovers of the fine arts and of Greece contributed to the degradation of the monuments.

First, by unearthing architectural blocks they provided some excellent material for the limekilns. As a result, the only evidence we have of the Corinthian capitals of Bassae, the earliest known example of the Corinthian order, comes from drawings made by the expedition.

Second, and this was another sign of the times, Thorvaldsen did not show the same respect for the marbles of Aegina that Canova had shown for the statues of the Parthenon. The Dane agreed to restore them in accordance with the taste of his time, thereby revealing that for him, at least, ancient statuary had an essentially ornamental role and that the art lover's pleasure took precedence over the demands of the scholar. However, a respect for authenticity was beginning to assert itself – neither the Elgin Marbles nor the *Venus de Milo* were restored.

Can one really justify the dismantling, in Munich, between 1966 and 1971, of the Danish sculptor's

Charles Robert Cockerell's drawing (below) gives a complete view of the discoveries made in the temple of Apollo Epikourios (the Helper) at Bassae, built at the end of the 5th century BC. The artist has distributed the most important pieces within the cella as required by the composition; Corinthian and Ionic capitals are given pride of place, as are the slabs of the interior frieze.

presentation? It corresponded to the taste of its period. Contemporary museum conservation favours origin at the expense of evolution, but art history is not necessarily the richer for it.

How do the Greeks react to the pillage?

To the Greeks, the statues that were unearthed on their soil possessed a magical value. The village elders went to ask Cockerell to stop the excavations, 'in order not to bring misfortune upon Aegina'.

Their fears were calmed by money they received. But payment could not negate an emerging national spirit, even if the spirit was not strong enough to have much force; it had not yet been instilled in the people. One should note, however, that efforts were made in that direction by the Society of Friends of the Muses, founded in Athens in 1813. The society's aims were to educate young people and to protect the antiquities.

And yet, alongside these negative aspects of the archaeological practices of the period, the scholarly study of Greece was being established. The Xeneion explored the country in every direction, amassing sketches and drawings. Haller von Hallerstein's drawings – only the views of Bassae have been preserved – display the architect's meticulous standards. They have nothing in common with the picturesque views of an artist like Julien David Le Roy. The monuments – every detail carefully marked and often commented upon – were ready for publication.

The Temple of Aegina, shown here in a reconstruction by Cockerell, had been visited by Jacob Spon in 1673 and drawn by Richard Chandler in 1765. The set of sculptures from the pediments revealed the existence of pre-classical sculpture, whicah, Haller von Hallerstein wrote, 'is dominated in every way by an awkward manner but an elevated spirit'.

The colour of art

The discoveries made by Haller von Hallerstein and his friends played an important role in two debates that rocked the scholarly world at the beginning of the 19th century: one issue was the roofing of the temples, and the other concerned the colour applied to statues and buildings by the Greeks. For a long time, in restorations of Greek temples an opening was left in the roof in order to light the cult statues or an interior frieze, as at Bassae. In a report of 1805–6, Quatremère de Quincy developed this idea at great length, even though it was erroneous in most cases (even at Bassae). In addition to this, he applied the principle in the transformations to which he subjected Soufflot's Panthéon, allowing light to pass through only the skylights.

And it was Quatremère de Quincy who set the tone in France on the question of the polychromy of Greek sculpture in his *Olympian Jupiter* of 1814, where he systematized a series of notations that had not hitherto been consistent. Still, he could not take into account observations made by Ludwig of Bavaria's agent or Cockerell concerning the marbles of Aegina, where the traces of paint were still clearly visible. While the debate on the subject of painted architecture was yet to occur, the polychromy of statues was already a well-documented fact.

In addition, by around 1820, considerable progress had been made in the understanding of Greek art. What was revealed by the originals from the workshops of Aegina, Phidias and Bassae (the *Venus de Milo* was thought to be by Praxiteles or from his studio) revolutionized knowledge of classical

This watercolour by Quatremère de Quincy depicts a group of statues in gold and ivory representing Poseidon and his wife, Amphitrite, in a chariot. The group was presented to the sanctuary of the Isthmus at Corinth by the wealthy Athenian Herodes Atticus, the tutor of the Roman emperor Marcus Aurelius. It is known only from Pausanias' description.

Greek art and showed that the time had come to rethink and revise totally the ideas on the history of art that had been propagated by Johann Joachim Winckelmann.

Greek neo-classicism

Even before its liberation in 1821, Greece, which was now better known, was at the centre of the debate about art and served as a reference for all those who defended classicism. It was the principles of the 'Greek style' that the Bavarian architect Leo von Klenze followed when designing the Glyptothek in Munich and other great buildings.

As early as 1790 in England, the Greek orders were fashionable. William Wilkins developed a style that was concerned with archaeological accuracy for Downing College in Cambridge, part of which was built between 1806 and 1811. Wilkins and Cockerell, respectively professor at the Royal Academy and president of the Royal Institute of Architects, completed the work of Stuart and Revett, the bible of the 'Greek Revival'. And then the liberation of Greece and the installation of a Bavarian monarchy in Athens brought about the dissemination of the Greek style in Greece itself.

After the victories of Germany over France, Ludwig I of Bavaria decided to build a monument in the form of a Greek temple to celebrate the great men of Germany. The sketch shown above is by Haller von Hallerstein, who was especially inspired by the proportions of the Parthenon. The monument was built by architect Leo von Klenze (1784–1864) between 1830 and 1842. The defeat of Napoleon at Leipzig and that of Augustus' general Varus in 9 AD by German tribesmen were depicted on the pediments.

Leo von Klenze summarizes what he knew about the topography of the Acropolis in this painting of 1846. In the foreground there is a picturesque scene on the Acropolis in which the Apostle Paul is preaching. Von Klenze came to Athens in 1834 as the Bavarian king's adviser on architecture. He wanted to create an archaeological storehouse to the north of the Acropolis, but his bold idea was not realized. He also undertook a comprehensive clearing of the Acropolis and a dismantling of all the medieval buildings on it.

"Brave and valiant Greeks, let us remember the ancient freedom of Greece, the battles of Marathon and Thermopylae; let us fight on the tombs of our ancestors who fell for the sake of our freedom."

Alexandros Ypsilantis, 1821

CHAPTER 6

THE TIME OF THE PALIKARS

The frontispiece (left) of the *Scholarly Expeditions to the Morea* (1831), where one can make out, at the foot of the caryatids, the fragments of the metopes of Olympia that are now in the Louvre. Opposite: a palikar, legendary fighter for Greek independence.

When the *Venus de Milo* arrived in Paris, the first uprisings in what was to be the war of liberation were taking place in Greece. That war would last for eight years. It mobilized international opinion through the information reported by the philhellenic committees, whose members included Byron, Elgin and Chateaubriand. Liberals and Christians were yearning for Greek independence and supported the revolt. The fierce and valiant fighters known as the palikars, who dressed in short full white skirts called fustanellas, became legendary characters, reviving the glory of Marathon; they were classical as well as Romantic heroes.

The struggle was long and bloody. The Greeks' early victories (1821–4) were followed by a successful Turkish counteroffensive (1824–7), which was brought to a halt by the destruction of the Turkish fleet at Navarino by the coalition of Great Britain, France and Russia. Independence was not definitively won until 1829. From 1827 to 1831 a Greek government, headed by Ioánnis Kapodistrias, who had been a minister for Czar Alexander I, attempted to organize the state. His assassination and the anarchy that ensued enabled the great powers to impose a Bavarian monarchy. King Otto entered Greece in 1832, at the age of seventeen, and he kept himself in power until 1862, when he was deposed by a liberal movement.

The Greeks recover their heritage

This period coincided with the time when the Greek nation regained control over its antiquities. The

"Here, in a few words, is the costume of a palikar of Athens [left]: a percale shirt with a large, folded-down collar; no tie; short cotton breeches, sometimes with stockings, always with gaiters done up to the knees – very similar to the greaves of Homer's warriors; red Oriental slippers; a fustanella (a very wide skirt) gathered at the waist; a belt and narrow garters of coloured silk; a sleeveless vest; a red hat with a blue tassel; a wide leather belt from which are hung an embroidered handkerchief, a purse, a tobacco pouch, a writing case and weapons. The vest and gaiters are almost always made of silk and are often embroidered with gold."

Edmond About
Contemporary Greece
1855

"When the king [Otto] crosses the streets of Athens in the costume of the palikar on a frisky horse that he leads gracefully, he can produce quite an illusion [left]. His height, his slim figure and a certain air of bored majesty have struck many foreigners who saw him from a distance. Europe has admired him from a distance for twenty years."

Edmond About
Contemporary Greece
1855

Greeks organized the first archaeological service and formulated legislation aimed at those who were preying on their treasures. The monuments of Athens, which was declared the capital city in 1833, were the focus of everybody's attention – the Greeks', as reminders of their former glory and independence, as well as the Germans', as the symbol of their newfound power. By the 1860s the generation of the palikars had disappeared; the period of the pioneers was followed by that of the writers and scholars.

The revolution had not spared the buildings. The Acropolis was occupied by a Turkish garrison, which was dislodged for the first time in 1822. Later, during the Turkish offensive in 1827, the Greeks were the victims of a violent siege in the course of which, according to one eyewitness, 180 bombs and 350 cannonballs were said to have fallen in a single day.

Clearly, when the Turks finally left the area, the buildings were in very bad condition; the western side of the Parthenon had suffered further damage and the Erechtheion had lost another of its caryatids. It may be noted, though, that the war had done no more damage there than Lord Elgin, who had already taken a caryatid to London.

The protection of antiquities

Amid all the difficulties associated with the creation of a state, the Greeks took steps to safeguard the antiquities: at a conference in 1827, they banned their export. It therefore took intense diplomatic efforts on the part of Kapodistrias himself, as well as the full weight of France's authority, at a time when the Greeks were negotiating a loan, for the Greek assembly to agree to

The *Apogee of Greece* by Karl Friedrich Schinkel (1781–1841) aroused a great deal of interest at a time when Greece was in the news (1825). Schinkel worked as an architect rather than as a painter, especially in Berlin, where he built in the neo-classical style. At the request of the court of Bavaria, he even designed a project for a royal palace on the Acropolis.

the French exporting the metopes of Olympia, now in the Louvre. These had been discovered by a scholarly expedition accompanying the French expeditionary force in the Morea that expelled the Turks.

Edgar Quinet, a young, enthusiastic and talented French Hellenist who later became the intellectual leader of mid-19th-century liberal thought in France, was sent as a member of the Morean expedition as an epigraphist. His book, *Modern Greece* (1830), was the product of his stay there; it was one of the last good books in the tradition of the picturesque travel accounts that Chateaubriand had helped to popularize.

The decline of the genre of accounts of travel to Greece was caused by their very abundance. All these picturesque narratives following the same itineraries became wearisome and dull; they were not, moreover, an appropriate means of scholarly publication, as the

Schinkel describes the moral value of this romantic and imaginary evocation of Athens: 'The landscape reveals the fullness of the culture of a remarkably well-educated people who knew how to make clever use of every element of nature to draw from it intense pleasure for the individual and, more generally, for the community. Through this picture, one can live with the people and follow them through all their purely human and political activities.'

German archaeologist Ludwig Ross pointed out in the introduction to his *Travels to the Islands*, one of the last classics of the genre, in 1835. The situation was changing. Increasingly, the most interesting publications on Greece were scholarly reports.

Organizing the archaeological service

From 1834 to 1836 Ross was the head of the newly created Archaeological Service, which was composed of regional authorities for continental Greece, the Peloponnese and the islands, and a central museum in the 'Theseion' of Athens. Initially, work centred on the ruins of the Acropolis where, in 1834, the German architect Leo von Klenze had one column of the Parthenon restored. To mark the symbolic value of the act, the column was decorated with myrtle and olive branches.

A year later the Bavarian garrison left the rock of the Acropolis and it came under the control of the Archaeological Service once and for all. The great concern of those years was the reconstruction of the small Temple of Athena Nike, all the blocks of which had been

The small Ionic Temple of Athena Nike (c. 430 BC) was still standing in 1676. It was demolished during the siege of 1687 to make way for a Turkish bastion. In 1835 three German archaeologists and architects began to rebuild it. The bas-reliefs and the north and south friezes had been carried off by Lord Elgin and were replaced by plaster casts.

Title page from the first edition of the journal of the Société Archéologique d'Athènes 1838 (right).

recovered from the Ottoman fortifications. The Acropolis was officially opened to the public in 1835 and its new fate as a tourist attraction was assured. Individual or family tickets were sold, allowing access for a period ranging from two days to nine months.

The Germans were not the only ones who were active at the time. Ludwig Ross, a young, gifted but arrogant scholar, was unwise enough to look down on his Greek superiors at the ministry, such as Alexander Rangabe, and his subordinates, such as Kyriakos Pittakis, who were both worthy representatives of the pioneering years of archaeology. Together the two Greeks decided to get rid of the haughty Ross, who held the chair of archaeology at the University of Athens until 1843. He was finally obliged to leave because a nationalist revolt was determined to remove foreigners and Greeks born outside Greece from positions in the administration.

Rangabe's collaboration with Kyriakos Pittakis was responsible for the creation of the first Greek archaeological review, *Ephemeris Archaiologiki*, and for the founding, also in 1837, of the Greek Archaeological Society – two institutions that still exist. They became landmarks of research in Greece, providing accommodation for members, whose dues were used to pay for excavations and to assemble antiquities, thereby making up for the state's lack of funds.

In 1842 Alexander Rangabe said that because of his zeal in the preservation of antiquities during the war, 'it is right to cite Mr K. Pittakis, the present director of the Museum of Athens [below]. With a palikar's rifle in his hand, he could be seen in those troubled times, looking for all the debris of antiquities, endangering his life to preservae them from the enemy's brutality, assembling them carefully and putting them into a safe place.'

French interests

Among foreign archaeologists, the French led initiatives in Greece, while the Germans, working from home or from Italy, laid the foundations of their great national collections.

France was responsible for two projects: expeditions for architects and the creation of a school for students of Greek civilization. Starting in 1845, the architects who were recipients of the Prix de Rome were invited to go and study the monuments of Greece; the ban on travel there was lifted after Quatremère de Quincy's death. This led to a series of very fine studies of the state of the sites and reconstructions of the monuments of Athens and Attica.

These artists stayed at the headquarters of the French School of Athens, which had been founded to house young Hellenists, with whom the artists sometimes collaborated. The French School was an original institution whose purpose was to contribute 'to the perfecting, for the study of the language, of Greek history and antiquities'; it was also supposed to reinforce the influence of France in Greece against that of the British colony at a time when the Greek

A detail of *The Sanctuary of Apollo on Delos*, a watercolour by Paul Nenot (above).

The Macedonian tomb of Pydna (seen in the lithographs below) was made up of a corridor, a Doric facade and a funerary chamber.

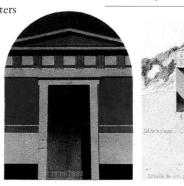

prime minister was decidedly sympathetic to French interests. The scholars, who stayed in Greece for two or three years, travelled around the country, read ancient poetry on the Acropolis, taught French and sometimes also did archaeological work.

German scholarship

Although they were less in evidence on Greek soil, German scholars were numerous and well-trained and occupied a growing number of university chairs; they were involved in two kinds of projects: drawing up catalogues of museums or collections and assembling collections of documents.

In 1829 an Institute of Archaeological Correspondence was created in Rome. This was an international association, led by Germans. Greece was involved in the institute's work in two ways. Scholars were sent to Athens to work on cataloguing inventories of the 'Theseion' and private collections. In addition, Eduard Gerhard, the guiding spirit of the institute, enabled vital progress to be made in the understanding of Greek vases, which had been found in vast numbers in 1828 in the Etruscan tombs at Vulci in Italy.

The colours of the architecture in these lithographs correspond to those actually used, unlike many reconstructions at the time. Above: decorative lion's heads adorned the four corners of the Parthenon's pediments.

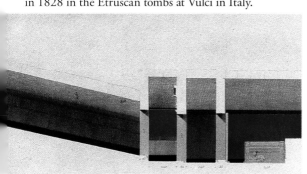

OLYMPIE

TEMPLE DE J...

COVPE - TRANSV...

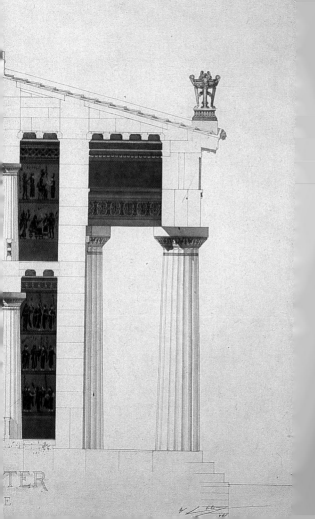

DES ... S D'APOLLON

ECHEL

The source of these vases (Corinth or Athens) was a subject of debate right up to the middle of the century. Nevertheless, the study of the inscriptions they bore proved conclusively that they had been imported into Italy from Greece and that they had not been produced locally, whether by Greeks or by others.

The Germans took a spectacular initiative regarding Greek inscriptions; the Academy of Berlin commissioned August Boeckh to bring together in one work all the inscriptions that had already been published – there were no fewer than six thousand. Regular revisions of the work were planned. From the time of the appearance of the first volume in 1825, the *Corpus* became an indispensable work.

German philology influenced all research. Thus, in sculpture, there was a loss of interest in 'the beautiful', as defined by Winckelmann; scholars began instead to go back to texts, such as those of Pliny the Elder, that described the works of the great masters and attempted to distinguish the famous originals from the numerous anonymous copies. This led to the recognition of the *Apoxyomenos* by Lysippos, the *Doryphoros* and the *Diadumenos* by Polyclitos, and the *Pluto, or Wealth, as an Infant in the Arms of Irene, or Peace* by Cephisodotos, the father of Praxiteles. It was this type of scholarly work that served as a guide for research until the beginning of the 20th century.

Ionians and Dorians

The discoveries of sculptures in Greece (the pediments of Aegina did not become well known until the Glyptothek was opened in 1830, just as the metopes of Olympia remained obscure until they were brought to the Louvre in 1829) fostered a debate concerning the great movements in Greek art. Under the influence of the German philologist and archaeologist Karl Otfried Müller and his theories about the Dorians, a contrast was established between a Dorian art and civilization (in Sparta and the Peloponnese) and an Ionian

This metope from the Temple of Zeus at Olympia (left) was transported to the Louvre after the Morean expedition. It shows Heracles in his struggle with the Cretan Bull. The geometric clarity of the composition and the expressive power of the hero's muscles are, according to some scholars, specific features of the Dorian aesthetic of the 460s BC.

The marble statue of an athlete cleaning himself with a scraper (opposite) was discovered in Rome in 1849 in the ruins of a house from the Imperial period. It was immediately recognized as a copy of the *Apoxyomenos* by Lysippos, a bronze statue described by Pliny the Elder. The original had been transported to Rome where, for a time, it was kept in the emperor Tiberius' bedroom.

art and civilization (in Athens, the Cyclades and Asia Minor). This division was not totally without justification, but the ethnic arguments for it were impossible to verify. That did not seem to matter.

The categories of Ionian art and Dorian art appeared to be quite distinct, and the discoveries of abundant archaic material at the end of the century served to reinforce convictions that had already become firmly entrenched.

The changing view of Greek art

At least until the 1850s, Greek art was elevated in scholarly circles to such an extent that Roman art was displaced. This enthusiasm also found its expression in the architecture of the period. Even though it was in decline in England from the 1830s, the Greek classical style remained fashionable for much longer in Scotland and Bavaria and lasted in Greece until about 1890. The Greek model was finally eclipsed at a time when the great excavations led to enormous progress in our understanding and knowledge of Greek art.

"It gives me great joy to announce to Your Majesty that I have discovered the tombs that have traditionally been known as the graves of Agamemnon, Cassandra, Eurymedon and their associates. In the tombs, I have found immense treasures consisting of archaic objects of pure gold."

Heinrich Schliemann to
George I, King of Greece, 1876

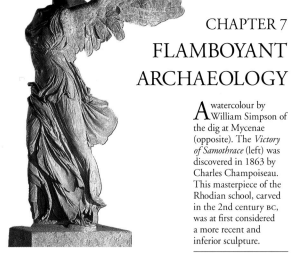

CHAPTER 7
FLAMBOYANT
ARCHAEOLOGY

A watercolour by William Simpson of the dig at Mycenae (opposite). The *Victory of Samothrace* (left) was discovered in 1863 by Charles Champoiseau. This masterpiece of the Rhodian school, carved in the 2nd century BC, was at first considered a more recent and inferior sculpture.

The great leap forward: the expansion of archaeology in Greece

What exactly is known about archaeology in Greece in the 1860s? Important discoveries were certainly made, but they covered only a small part of the historic terrain. There still had not been systematic excavations of any site; archaeologists had been satisfied to scratch the ground in a sporadic fashion looking for museum pieces. No complete topographical map had yet been drawn of a city or a sanctuary. Greek and foreign scholars were therefore exploring almost completely virgin territory. In the space of half a century, they increased our knowledge to such an extent that we have still not drawn all the necessary conclusions from their work, and we are still publishing their discoveries.

This expansion of Greek archaeology, which profited from the development of history and geography and the new appetite for knowledge that characterized these disciplines, was essentially led by academics. However, in this pioneering period, Greek archaeology also aroused the interest of such outstanding individuals as Heinrich Schliemann and Sir Arthur John Evans.

In *The King of the Mountains* (1856), French journalist Edmond About humorously castigates Greek bandits; Gustave Doré's illustrations (above) helped immensely to make the book a success. About's scholarly work on Aegina aroused mixed reactions.

A country suffering political upheaval, invaded by archaeologists

It was truly a pioneering epoch, since working in Greece was still dangerous, so unstable was the social and political situation there. Even in the environs of Athens, archaeologists had to be escorted by soldiers. And, even taking such precautions, in 1870 a group of Englishmen and Italians fell into the hands of bandits. The emotion aroused by the murder of these gentlemen was intense. As late as 1909 the preface to the *Guide Joanne* (the ancestor of the *Blue Guide*) had to reassure travellers about safety, which, it claims, had improved considerably in twenty years! It was still not a good idea to visit the frontier provinces, especially the Greek territories that were under Turkish control, where constant unrest was endemic.

There was widespread support in Greece for the 'Great Idea', which aimed to unite Greece with all the territories that had a Greek majority population. Through the adjudication of other countries, Greece thus recovered the Heptanesos, or the seven Ionian Islands, under British protection, in 1864 and Thessaly in 1881. Crete, which

This scene, showing clandestine digging at Corinth in 1877, could also illustrate the activity of the robbers of antiquities in Boeotia, where more than eight thousand tombs were opened from 1870 to 1873. They revealed, most notably, hundreds of Hellenistic terracotta statuettes now known as Tanagra figurines.

had won autonomy in 1897, was attached to the kingdom in 1912 and Macedonia was first partitioned in 1913. It would be false to claim that such progress in the liberation of Greece was inspired by a powerful philhellenic spirit, as had been the case at the start of the 19th century.

The French philhellenes, who formed a league in 1904, did not number more than twenty at their first meeting. 'Hellenism has to be defended, and it deserves to be defended, whatever determined adversaries or disillusioned friends may argue against the Greeks. It is important, for the balance of power in the East and in the common interest of Europe, that it be defended,' states the league's charter.

In this complex question of the Near East, archaeology played an often unwarranted role in supporting the territorial demands of the Balkan nations. At the same time, the great powers, especially France and Germany, after the Franco-Prussian War of 1870, added research in Greece to the fields in which they were rivals.

Delphic disputes: an international saga of raisins and blackmail

The story of awarding the excavation of Delphi to the French provides a colourful illustration of the international and local conditions of archaeological work in Greece. The Germans were able to assert their rights to Delphi, where Müller had led excavations in 1840. But in 1861 and 1880 the French had taken an interest in the polygonal wall that supported the terrace of the temple upon which many inscriptions were

At Delphi, the Sanctuary of Apollo was covered by the village of Kastri. Théophile Homolle, the future director of the French School, said: 'Are you at Delphi? The conquest of the polygonal wall will take three times as long and will cost no fewer assaults, labourers and schemes than the conquest of the walls of Troy.' The Frenchman Paul Fournier is seen copying the inscriptions of the polygonal wall in 1896 (left).

engraved. They demanded the right to work on the site, where, since the process took so long, the German Hans Pomtow still managed to excavate in 1887.

The Greek prime minister, the very competent Kharílaos Trikoúpis, thought of linking the rights to the site to favourable customs terms for the raisins the French imported from Corinth. Faced with the French refusal to give in to this commercial blackmail, he offered the excavation to the Germans. Some scholars pointed out in a collegial spirit that it might not be appropriate for the French to excavate Delphi, as they had just ransacked Delos. But the Academy of Berlin politely turned down Trikoúpis' offer. The Americans, who had recently arrived in Greece, were also involved, but eventually the French won the day without having to give way on the

The discoveries at Delphi were superb. The *Charioteer* (above), one of the few surviving Greek bronzes, was unearthed at the same time as one of the blocks of its base, shown in the foreground of the photograph above left. The inscription reveals that this statue belonged to a group dedicated by a tyrant from Sicily on the occasion of a victory at the Pythian Games in the 470s BC.

raisins – though not without some outlay. The entire village of Kastri, built over the site and consisting of a thousand houses, had to be bought – for 500,000 gold francs – and rebuilt. The inhabitants were furious at the violence being done to them and rebelled; digging began in 1892, under the protection of an armed force. Fortunately for the French, the discoveries justified the large investment.

The proliferation of foreign schools: German, French, American, British and Austrian

Foreign states did not derive any material benefit from such costly enterprises; the Greek constitution forbade the export of antiquities. The Germans were legitimately proud of having signed the first convention of 'disinterested' excavations with the Greeks in 1875, in return for the rights to the site of Olympia; all that was found would remain in Greece, and only duplicates could be exported. Otto von Bismarck, the German chancellor, was not taken in by this and cut the budget in 1881. However, the kaisers understood better than the chancellor the prestige that could be derived from archaeology. They financed excavations from their own resources: Wilhelm I financed those of Olympia and his grandson those of Corfu. As for the French, they saw that archaeology was so much in their interest that

French architects and archaeologists (below) in front of the headquarters of the excavations of Delos in 1910. The clearing of the Sanctuary of Apollo on Delos began in 1873; work was particularly intense between 1904 and 1914. It proved possible to restore a sanctuary and bring life back to a city of the 2nd to 1st centuries BC.

they opened a section to admit foreign students.

Prosperous nations wanted to follow France and Germany's example. In 1882 the Americans and in 1885 the British created their own independent establishments. However, since these were foundations that relied essentially upon private funds, they were less tied to the interests of the state. Later, the Austrians (1898) and the Italians (1909) opened their own institutes, whose means were, however, in no way comparable to those enjoyed by the French or Germans. The last third of the 19th century was thus marked by a proliferation of foreign schools and excavations.

The sites of the major excavations

A geography of excavations – which has scarcely been modified at all to this day – was established. Since before 1914, to mention only the major excavations, the French worked at Delphi, Delos, Thasos and Argos (the city); the Germans worked at Olympia, on the Kabeirion of Thebes, on Samos and in the Kerameikos of Athens; the Americans at Corinth and in the Heraion of Argos; the British in the Peloponnese (Megalopolis and Sparta); the Italians in Crete (Gortyna, Ida, Phaistos); and the Austrians in Samothrace (these sites were later taken over by the Americans).

Workers on the Greek excavations in the Byzantine monastery of Daphnē in 1891 (above). The monuments of the Middle Ages did not immediately attract the attention of scholars, who demolished them whenever they interfered with the prominence of more ancient buildings (the Parthenon, Hadrian's Library). In the 1890s, however, the Greeks began excavating and restoring Daphnē's 11th-century mosaics.

It should also be said that even though the metopes in the Louvre gave some idea of the sculpted decoration of Olympia, the discovery of the pediments revealed the mastery of Peloponnesian sculptors in the 460s BC.

And yet what marked this period was not so much the discoveries as the revelation of civilizations about which written tradition had been silent or of periods that had left only fleeting traces in literature: the Geometric Period (from the 10th to the 8th centuries BC), the Mycenaean civilization, the Minoan civilization, the culture of the Cyclades, the Neolithic sites of Thessaly, Sesklo and Dimini. Greece's past was, in effect, extended by several millennia. In this journey back through time, preeminent roles were played by two very different characters: Heinrich Schliemann, a merchant from Mecklenburg, a self-taught archaeologist with a vivid imagination, and Sir Arthur John Evans, a great liberal gentleman, who had been educated at Oxford and was a disciplined scholar. They were alike only in their passion for the archaeology of the early periods and in the way they invested their fortunes in the excavations they organized in Greece.

Heinrich Schliemann, a man of myth and scandal

Schliemann pursued a coherent plan of research that led him to Ithaca in 1868 and then to Turkey, to the site of Hissarlik, in 1872 to 1873. He proved that this was the site of the ancient city of Troy and unearthed fabulous jewelry, which was immediately named Priam's Treasure, the jewels of the beautiful Helen. He brought that treasure back from Turkey to Greece and became embroiled in a sensational legal dispute initiated by the Turkish government, and he was obliged to buy his way out of the situation.

In Mycenae in 1874, an error in Pausanias' text led Schliemann to discover a circle of

Heinrich Schliemann (below left), the son of a pastor, succeeded in commerce because of his gift for languages and his lack of scruples. In 1868, having made his fortune, he went on a world tour and decided to devote his life to the search for the world of Homer. This conversion to Hellenism included a Greek marriage to Sophie Schliemann, who is shown above, wearing the jewels Schliemann found at Troy.

The Lion Gate, Mycenae, 1250 BC. These reflections by Schliemann on the excavations of Olympia reveal his views: 'They do everything in reverse; they remove one layer after another. They will spend an infinite amount of time and money there; one must go immediately to the core, and then one discovers it.' The Schliemanns, by themselves, supervised about 120 workers at Mycenae and had various disputes with the representatives of the Greek Archaeological Service.

graves inside the Acropolis; he excavated five of them, in accordance with the text of Pausanias' *Description of Greece*, but he overlooked the sixth, which he was not expecting to find (and which would later be discovered by the Greeks). He revealed to the scholarly world as well as to the general public the extraordinary treasures of a civilization that had been forgotten until then: funerary masks made of gold, gold and bronze cups, headbands, damascened daggers, tomb slabs bearing ancient sculpted reliefs. All this was promptly exhibited and published in German and in English. Schliemann then returned to Troy, and in 1881 he offered his portion of the finds he had made, including Priam's Treasure,

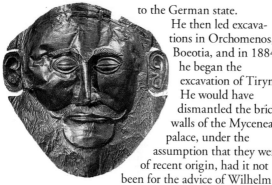

to the German state. He then led excavations in Orchomenos, Boeotia, and in 1884 he began the excavation of Tiryns. He would have dismantled the brick walls of the Mycenean palace, under the assumption that they were of recent origin, had it not been for the advice of Wilhelm Dörpfeld, the first secretary of the German Institute of Athens. Schliemann had been collaborating with Dörpfeld since 1882. Some people have said – not entirely without justification – that Schliemann's finest discovery was actually Dörpfeld.

It should also be said that Schliemann had what would today be called a sense of the media. He did not shrink from employing any means of making himself known around the world – organizing exhibitions, lectures and publications in every European language. He even asked William Gladstone, the British prime minister, to write the preface to his book about Mycenae in 1878. By ensuring his own fame, he also served the interests of Greek archaeology and those of Greece itself. He also had two masterpieces of the late-19th-century neo-classical style built in Athens, his house and his tomb.

One of the five gold masks (left) from the wealth of objects in the tombs discovered by Schliemann at Mycenae (from the 16th century BC). The masks were produced by pressing a sheet of gold into shape over a wooden sculpture. This material was quite unique. There is no known equivalent in the Aegean to this first attempt at royal portraiture. Just as exceptional are the stelae decorated with scenes of war and hunting that marked the tombs.

Wilhelm Dörpfeld, whose head is emerging from this vessel, was the first of those remarkable architect-archaeologists who made the German school unique. Trained in the pioneering excavations at Olympia, he directed the German Institute from 1887 to 1912. Since he was especially open to such new techniques as stratigraphy and photography, he had the best possible influence on Schliemann. He conducted research in Athens and in Leukas.

Sir Arthur John Evans: a scholar in the house of Minos

Schliemann's and Evans' paths crossed at Knossos: Schliemann was unable to acquire the land, but Evans succeeded, with the help of Ioseph Hatzidakis, who was in charge of archaeology and education in the independent government of Crete. The discovery of the Minoan civilization was thus made by a Briton. Evans had the advantage over Schliemann of being a cultivated heir to a fortune. While Schliemann represented the conquering spirit of the travelling salesman, Evans represented a prosperous Britain that was enjoying the fruits of the industrial revolution. Evans went to Greece in 1893. In antiques shops in Athens he found engraved stones that came from Crete and bore hieroglyphic signs – the earliest revelation of Minoan writing. Evans decided to begin excavating at Knossos. He paid for the land from his own pocket and dug the first spadeful of earth in 1899. That was how he came to make the extraordinary discovery of the palace of Minos.

How can one fail to admire this great British scholar who, not content to reveal a new civilization, was able to establish chronologies of Minoan Crete and also of the

The north entrance to the Palace of Knossos (above). The palace covered 13,000 square metres (the largest in Crete). Rooms were arranged around a central courtyard of 1250 square metres, where religious ceremonies and bull contests were held. This striking architecture, with its many corridors and floors, together with the ritual importance of bulls, inspired the myth of the labyrinth and the Minotaur.

This detail (left) comes from a fresco at the Palace of Knossos. Sir Arthur Evans (below, at Knossos) travelled the world as a journalist and embraced the cause of the new Slavic nations, which led to his being imprisoned in 1882. After his return to England, his career as an archaeologist began when he was made curator of the Ashmolean Museum in Oxford, which he enriched with his personal collections.

Cyclades in the third and early second millennia BC, chronologies that are still in use today? He was also the last scholar to be able to satisfy his archaeologist's passion in his own right in Greece. The era of the pioneers was definitely over.

The prestige of archaeology: the world's interest is awakened

Before the First World War, Greek archaeology was quite international and so extremely productive, but it was also distinctly divided. The foreign institutes in Greece did not share any common plan, and there was not a single joint excavation undertaken by Greeks and foreigners. Each group jealously watched over its digs and independently sought glory for itself.

In 1886, for instance, on the hundredth anniversary of the first exhibition of fine arts in Berlin, the Germans reconstructed the facade of the temple of Olympia in its true dimensions, and the temple was placed on a terrace decorated with plaster casts of the Pergamum frieze.

Just as the Reich celebrated its archaeological triumphs, France glorified the work the French were doing in Greece. At the Universal Exposition of 1889, the archaeologist Théophile Homolle spoke of the excavations at Delos. A cast of the sphinx from the Monument of the Naxians, recently discovered at Delphi, was exhibited at the Exposition of 1900.

Even the Greeks themselves profited from their heritage: in 1896, Athens staged the first modern Olympic Games.

Modern art abandons Greece, turning to other sources

Interest in archaeology and in classical culture remained alive in Europe and attracted foreigners to Greece. The German travel guide (*Baedeker*) and the French travel guide (*Joanne*) were written by archaeologists and still serve as useful handbooks. The curiosity of academics and tourists replaced the enthusiasm of artists, who had turned away from the canons of classicism: Post-Impressionist Paul Cézanne denounced the imitation of the Greeks and Romans as pernicious, even though, on an earlier occasion, he had expressed his admiration for the masterpieces in the Louvre. In 1909 the Futurists declared that 'a racing car is more beautiful than the *Victory of Samothrace*', while members of the Dada movement suggested placing splints on the *Venus de Milo* and proposed 'letting Laocoön and his children rest after their thousand-year-long struggle with that fine sausage of a serpent, Python'.

And yet, classical culture did not collapse beneath the weight of such sarcastic comments. It was not until the late 1960s that drawing from plaster casts of antique sculptures ceased to be a privileged exercise in many art schools, and it took just as long for ancient culture to stop being the favoured subject of the elite in the field of education.

Poster for the first modern Olympic Games, held in Athens in 1896.

"If the 19th century has to be considered in the history of the ancient world as the century of systematic research, of the ordering of the 'archives of the past', what took place in the first half of the 20th century was the start of an increased awareness and examination of the problems they posed, a constant effort to grasp the object of art in its intrinsic value."

Ranucchio Bianchi-Bandinelli, 1978

CHAPTER 8
A TIME OF MATURE REFLECTION

Archaeologist Fred Boissonas (opposite) on a ladder facing the Parthenon. The *Bronze Jockey* (left, 2nd century BC), was found in 1928 on a shipwrecked vessel off Euboea. He was put back onto his horse at the National Archaeological Museum in Athens.

The effects of the First World War on archaeology in Greece

The First World War did not cause archaeological work to be interrupted; in fact, in some ways, it acted as a stimulus. The Franco-British expeditionary corps that occupied northern Greece after landing in Gallipoli in 1915 included an archaeological team. It was this team that began the excavation of prehistoric sites in Macedonia. Archaeologists with the Eastern army died on the battlefield. At the end of the war, the treaties extended the area open to archaeology by granting Thrace to Greece. But the Dodecanese had come under Italian control in 1912, which is why the policy concerning excavation in Rhodes and Kos was decided in Rome until the fall of Mussolini's regime.

As for the German Institute of Athens, which was shut down by the Allies in 1916, it had no difficulty in opening again as early as 1920 – such was the prestige enjoyed by German scholarship. However, a minor incident revealed the tensions that existed between the victors and the vanquished in the immediate postwar period. A German professor who had been sent to Athens to negotiate the institute's reopening wanted to excavate in the vicinity of the Monument of Lysicrates. France protested, claiming rights to that area that went back to the opening of a Capuchin monastery on the site in 1669. Excavations were eventually resumed by the Greeks themselves.

A time of cutbacks

The political and economic situation, both international and local, had various repercussions on archaeological work in Greece. Greece fought in Turkey until 1922 and then had to employ all its resources to shelter the 1.5 million refugees from Asia Minor. All this meant that there was little money for archaeology. In addition, the atmosphere of the archaeological world was disturbed by political compromises. In 1920 force had to be used yet again to expel the overzealous royalist Panagiotis Kavvadias from his post as secretary of the archaeological society, which he had held again since 1912. Fortunately

The statuary group consisting of Boreas, the North Wind, abducting Orithyia, an Athenian princess, stood at the top of the Temple of the Athenians on Delos. This photograph is by Fred Boissonas (1858–1946), who produced a series of books on Greece that are full of fascinating photographs.

for the society, Giorgos Oikonomos, an experienced archaeologist who was more moderate in his opinions, was the director of the National Archaeological Museum in Athens from 1930 to 1933. He was promoted to positions of authority in the ministry from 1933 to 1938. He was secretary of the archaeological society from 1924 to 1951 and managed to maintain a certain equilibrium in the archaeological domain in spite of the unstable political situation: democracy (1924–35), return to monarchy (1936–41), several attempts at dictatorship, and the war, with foreign military occupation from 1941 to 1944.

If working conditions were thus not at all favourable for the Greeks, the consequences of the First World War and the world economic crisis of 1929 also affected the foreign schools, whose budgets were cut. In some cases, wealthy sponsors, or *evergetes*, made up the shortfall; these included Gustav Oberländer, who gave the Germans money in order to continue work at the Kerameikos in Athens, and John D. Rockefeller, who helped the Americans to open the Athenian Agora.

Semni Papaspyridi joined the Greek Archaeological Service in 1921 after studying in Athens and Munich. She held posts at Nauplia and at the National Archaeological Museum in Athens in the department of ceramics. After her marriage she took part in the postwar reorganization of the museum. A scholar of international repute, she was an important personality in Greek archaeology.

Women archaeologists

Another sign of the times was that women were playing a much greater role in Greek archaeology. A number of young female academics had been sent to Athens as early as 1890, but they had not taken part in the excavations. Then, between the two world wars, they led work in the field, and the American teams working on the Agora included women. The Greeks were not left behind in this respect since, in 1921, Semni Papaspyridi (later Mrs Karouzou), one of the great ladies of archaeology, was taken on by the archaeological service after a competitive selection process. Thus began a more equal representation of the sexes in the field of archaeology, which has continued ever since.

The objects of study and the study of objects

In spite of various difficulties, there were still many excavations in progress. And even though the discoveries did not cause the stir that Schliemann's and Evans' had, they were often extremely interesting and of very high quality. For example, in 1924, in the Minoan palace of

The marbles of Olympia (below, the Apollo from the west pediment of the temple) were restored for the Berlin Olympics in 1936. That was also when the excavations of Olympia were reopened. Thus archaeology played a role in Nazi propaganda.

Atlas portrayed by the Athena Painter (opposite).

Mallia, the French discovered some extraordinary weapons, including a long bronze sword with a crystal hilt and gold ornamentation. When the Germans reopened the excavations of the Heraion on Samos in 1925 they found many archaic objects. In 1935 the Greeks excavated a sanctuary dating from the 7th century BC at Dreros, in Crete, that still contained statues of a primitive triad of Apollo, Artemis and Leto. When one of the slabs on the Sacred Way at Delphi was lifted, a ditch full of precious offerings made in the sanctuary and then discarded was discovered.

A calmer time, an age of reflection

This was, however, no longer the turbulent time of great excavations and marvellous discoveries. The 1920s and '30s were more an age of mature reflection and of publication. What characterized the scholarly output of the time was the study of objects and monuments, both individually and as series.

It was while researching archaic statues that the Englishman Humphrey Payne placed the torso of a kore that had been in Lyons since 1810 back onto her legs, which had remained in Athens, and attached the head of an aristocrat from the 530s–520s BC that belonged to the Louvre to the bust of a horseman that had been found on the Acropolis. Chronologies were made more precise, the technical understanding of objects was improved, corpuses were assembled and handbooks were written.

All this work was evidence of an astonishing erudition and revealed quite extraordinary talents. In 1925 an Englishman, John Beazley, was able to attribute ten thousand vases or fragments of vases to two hundred different painters; by 1942 he had studied fifteen thousand vases and recognized the hand of eight hundred painters. His outstanding work won him a well-deserved knighthood.

Less progress was made in the theory of art. The fine archaeologist Ernst Buschor, who wrote a general work on the subject, was still very much attached to an idealist view. For him, sculpture had to undergo certain fixed phases of development, whatever the type of civilization in which it

The *Rampin Head* belongs to a horseman whose torso was found on the Acropolis in Athens with part of his horse. The crown of oak leaves is associated with a victory in an equestrian contest.

was produced. The link between the production of forms and images and a society was of little or no interest.

Ideas and ideologies in peril

Several more or less dangerous myths continued to circulate. Evans, whose definitive publications on the Palace of Knossos appeared between 1921 and 1935, did not wish to give up the idea that Crete had had a permanent influence on the mainland. On the other hand, A. J. B. Wace, who had begun excavations in Mycenae in 1921, defined the specific features of Mycenaean civilization and its originality in relation to the Minoan world. It was only the deciphering of the tablets written in Linear B from 1952 onwards that completely overturned that perspective by proving that the Greeks had occupied Knossos from as early as 1400 BC.

There was another debate, in the Schliemann tradition, that still continued to obscure our knowledge of the Greek world: the debate concerning Homeric geography. Victor Bérard, the eminent Hellenist who published a French translation of the *Odyssey*, claimed to have found the true sites that Odysseus had passed through, and he went on a tour of the Mediterranean in order to identify them. What remains from that rather perilous venture, since the *Odyssey* is by no means a travel guide, is a fine album of photographs taken by Fred Boissonas, who accompanied Bérard on his voyage.

Finally, there was still a tendency in art history to contrast Ionians with Dorians and to base the contrasts between the artistic schools of Asia Minor or of the Peloponnese on ethnic criteria. This debate went back to Karl Otfried Müller's book *The Dorians*, published in 1824; it took an extremely racist turn with a number of scholars who were taken in by Nazi ideology and considered that the Dorians belonged to a 'superior' Nordic race. It was in this context that one must view the reopening of the excavations of Olympia at the same time as the Olympic Games were being held in Berlin in 1936. It was not merely sport that provided the link and led the organizers to fetch the symbolic flame from Olympia; race was also involved, since Olympia and

The upper part of this statue is mentioned as being in a private collection in Marseilles in 1719. It entered the Musée des Beaux-Arts in Lyons in 1810. Thought to be a Gallo-Roman Isis, an Athena with an owl or an Aphrodite with a dove, it is in fact a kore from the mid-6th century BC. Its lower part was found on the Acropolis.

The clearing of the ancient Athenian Agora (opposite, above, at the foot of the Hephaisteion), like that of the Roman Agora (opposite, below), was first undertaken by the Greek Archaeological Society, but only limited excavation could be carried out since the land was occupied by inhabited houses. With the financial support of John D. Rockefeller, the American School had to rehouse five thousand people before it was able to unearth the political centre of ancient Athens. The rubble covering the archaeological layers was between one and a dozen metres deep, depending on the location. It was not until the 1970s that the areas to the north of the square were purchased and excavated, these being unfortunately divided by the railway line between Athens and Piraeus.

Sparta were the centres of Dorism. Nor did the German Archaeological Institute of Athens remain free of Nazism, since its director from 1936, Walther Wrede, was also the head of the National Socialist organization in Greece. But other professional German archaeologists managed to limit the archaeological activity of those teams that were directly dependent on the 'Amt Rosenberg'; apart from plundering artworks, this organization had a scholarly purpose and hoped to find, in Greece, as a result of the Dorian invasions, traces of the civilization of the 'Nordic masters'. The myth of Nordic and triumphant Dorism collapsed with the fall of Nazi Germany.

New approaches

Certain innovative projects that prefigured postwar archaeology should be mentioned here. Ernst Langlotz renewed the approach to Greek art by attempting to distinguish regional styles in original bronze statuettes; he thus broke with the study of the 'great' masters and the reconstruction of their work from copies.

In fact, it was by being concerned with more than the search for fine objects and by taking into account all archaeological finds as evidence of a material civilization that archaeology could contribute to a better understanding of ancient Greece. In this regard, the American excavations of the Agora, which began in 1931, were exemplary. Even the most humble objects were of interest there – simple kitchen utensils, modest, undecorated terracotta lamps, amphorae that had been used to store oil or wine. It was with this same attitude that another American team worked at Olynthos, in Chalcidice. The publication of the inventories of this set of houses includes all categories of objects, even pinheads. Moreover, domestic architecture, a field in which the French led the way in Delos, now received the same attention as the products of monumental, public or, especially, sacred architecture.

The tendencies that have come to predominate in the second half of the 20th century were thus beginning to be defined: a desire to conduct exhaustive studies, an interest in the small potsherd as well as the beautiful

artifact and attention paid to vernacular architecture as well as temples or porticoes.

After the Second World War two revolutions took place, both of them in the 1950s: a technical revolution – the introduction of 'stratigraphic' methods of excavation that enabled any object to be placed within an archaeological layer; and a crucial discovery – the decipherment of Linear B, which put an end to a large number of myths.

Quite recently, such sensational discoveries as the frescoes of Thera and the Macedonian royal tombs prove the inexhaustible richness of Greek archaeology, but they also partly mask the decisive but unspectacular progress that has been made in our understanding of Greece, progress that may itself be obscuring problems and difficulties to be faced tomorrow.

Excavations at the site of Akrotiri (Thera), begun in 1870 and continued in 1967, have yielded fabulous treasures, including a storeroom with large jars in place (above) and (overleaf) a fresco of two boxers.

DOCUMENTS

Was Santorini Plato's mythical Atlantis?

In 1967 Spyridon Marinatos, an archaeologist and professor at the University of Athens, began to uncover the remains of a sophisticated civilization on the island of Santorini. The island, which had been destroyed by a volcanic eruption in the 16th century BC, contained ruins evocative of the Minoan civilization of Crete. What were the consequences of the volcanic eruption in the Aegean Sea? Is there a link between it, the destruction of the Cretan palaces and the myth of the lost continent that Plato described?

The destruction occurs in several stages

Towards the end of the 16th century BC, the city of Akrotiri was destroyed and the entire island of Santorini was buried beneath a thick layer of volcanic ash. Judging by the archaeological evidence, the events transpired as follows.

Some time before the eruption of the volcano, the city suffered considerable damage, most likely due to a series of earthquakes; when these were over, systematic work was undertaken to clear the streets of rubble, to demolish walls that were in danger of collapsing and to repair the houses. However, while this work was still going on, the volcano began to erupt, and the inhabitants were obliged to leave the city. Probably they had been alerted by the appearance of smoke and toxic gases. Before fleeing, they carefully stored their stocks of foodstuffs safely beneath the floors. When evacuating the city, they took all their valuables with them. This explains the total absence of bodies and precious objects buried beneath the ruins.

In the course of the first, minor, eruption, fine pellets of pumice stone covered not only the city but the entire island, forming a hermetic coating approximately three cm thick. This coating constituted an end of all human activity. The oxidation of this layer of pumice stone suggests that for a period of time of not more than two years, according to the experts, the volcano remained completely inactive. It was after this period that the principal eruption took place; it occurred in several stages. Pumice stone accumulated in several phases to a depth of about six metres in some

H ousing area, Akrotiri, Santorini.

tidal wave it caused directly influenced the end of the Minoan civilization on Crete. Similarly, few people still defend the historicity of the myth of Atlantis.

Much has been said about the discoveries made in Akrotiri and their possible links with the legend of Atlantis. It is true that some aspects of the discoveries made on Santorini are similar to the description given by Plato of some parts of Atlantis.

For example, the impressive buildings with walls of white or brown volcanic stones resemble the buildings he describes. The art of Akrotiri and the high standard of life that it reflects correspond to the description Plato gives of Atlantis. And the corrected date of the disappearance of Atlantis, c. 1500 BC, coincides perfectly with that of the eruption on Santorini. Nevertheless, despite all the credit that one may attribute to Plato's descriptions, many other features do not correspond.

Plato was a political philosopher whose objective was to institute a system that would, in his opinion, be profitable to Athenian society. His model of the ideal city state (Atlantis), destroyed by the gods because its citizens neglected the principles Plato wanted to inculcate into his fellow citizens, cannot be based on literal truth. And it is indeed strange and interesting to note that no other ancient author mentions the city of Atlantis or even makes any allusion to it.

Christos Doumas
La Recherche, no. 143, 1983

Christos Doumas, professor of prehistoric archaeology at the University of Athens, has directed excavations on Santorini since 1974.

places; then enormous amounts of volcanic ash fell, forming a layer more than thirty metres thick in some areas. In addition to the ash, the volcano threw out enormous blocks of ancient rock, which broke away from the walls of the crater. After this eruption, life on the island ceased altogether. Archaeological evidence does not reveal any human presence for the next two centuries.

Ash originating from the eruption has been found on Melos, Crete, Rhodes and Kos. However, largely for chronological reasons, it is no longer believed that the eruption or the

The earliest known form of Greek

At the beginning of the 20th century, Sir Arthur Evans distinguished three types of writing on Crete. One, resembling Egyptian hieroglyphs, was in use c. 2000–1650 BC; another was made up of simple lines and was therefore referred to as Linear A (1750–1450 BC); and the third, Linear B, did not appear until approximately 1400 BC.

In 1952 a young Englishman, Michael Ventris (1922–56), showed that Linear B was a very archaic form of Greek. With John Chadwick, professor of Greek at Cambridge University, he undertook to decipher the clay tablets on which the accounts of the Mycenaean palaces were inscribed. It was a revolutionary step that had two important consequences. It showed that Knossos had been under Greek domination since 1400 BC and that the world of Homer really had nothing in common with that of the Mycenaean palaces – as a small number of scholars, including M. I. Finley (in his book, The World of Odysseus, *which appeared in 1954), had already realized.*

A prodigy

In 1940 a new name appears in the literature of [the archaeology of Crete]: Michael Ventris, then only eighteen years old. His article 'Introducing the Minoan Language' was published in the *American Journal of Archaeology;* in

writing to the editor he had been careful to conceal his age, but although in later years he dismissed the article as 'puerile', it was nonetheless soundly written. His basic idea was to find a language which might be related to Minoan. Ventris' candidate was Etruscan – not a bad guess because, according to ancient tradition, the Etruscans came from the Aegean to Italy. Ventris attempted to see how the Etruscan language would fit with Linear B. The results, as he admitted, were negative, but the Etruscan idea remained a fixation that possessed him until the Greek solution finally came to him in 1952.... At this date Greek seemed out of the question. 'The theory that Minoan could be Greek', Ventris wrote, 'is based of course upon a deliberate disregard for historical plausibility.' Hardly anyone would have ventured to disagree.

Tablet written in Linear B.

Ventris announces his discovery on the BBC

'During the last few weeks, I have come to the conclusion that the Knossos and Pylos tablets must, after all, be written in Greek – a difficult and archaic Greek, seeing that it is 500 years older than Homer and written in a rather abbreviated form, but Greek nevertheless.' (*The Listener*, 10 July 1952)

I do not think it can be said that this broadcast made a great impression; but I, for one, was an eager listener. In view of the recurrent claims that had been made, I did not regard Ventris' system as standing much chance.

John Chadwick
The Decipherment of Linear B, 1967

Chadwick contacted Ventris, and this was the start of a friendship and the definitive decipherment of Linear B; their collaboration came to an end with Ventris' early death in 1956.

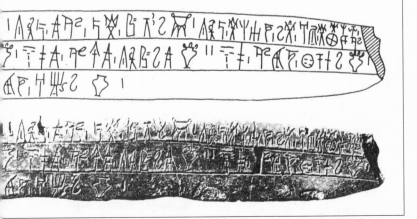

Rome pillages Greece

In 1972 near Riace, Calabria, two statues made of bronze were discovered in the sea. Scholars agree that they are classical Greek originals that had been taken from Greece and were being transported to Italy. But many questions remain. When were these bronzes shipped to Italy? To which monuments did they belong? Who created them, and when?

Finding the bronzes

Credit for the discovery is due to S. Mariottini, a chemist from Rome who was on holiday at Monasterace Marina, a few miles from Riace. On the morning of 16 August 1972, on an underwater fishing trip with two cousins, while diving near the submerged cliff at the spot known as Porto Farticchio, opposite the Agranci estate in Riace Marina, he saw 'something that vaguely resembled a human elbow and an arm'. Digging into the sand, he uncovered the bronze statue to which the arm belonged, and he found another one a short distance away. Leaving a marker balloon at the site, Mariottini came back to the spot that afternoon and dived with his relatives; he could now clearly see the importance of the discovery.

Claudio Sabbione
'Due Bronzi da Riace'
in *Bolletino d'Arte*, 1984

How to look at bronzes

As far as we know, Nero was the last person to bring statues (the Odysseus of the group by Onatas, for example) from Greece to Rome. The philhellenism of Domitian and Hadrian was expressed in different ways. In short, it is quite probable that Pausanias did not see the statues of Riace. To look for them in his text would be to commit an error of method. It would make useless a large part of the writings that they have inspired.

When making judgments about them, we have only the statues themselves to go on. The problem to be resolved in identifying them and giving them a location is therefore that of the typology of statue A, that is, the

A

B

The Riace bronzes.

joint presence of the headband and shield. Apart from this, one has to consider the features that are either certain or probable:

• The two statues are in the Attic style, one dating from 460 BC, the other from 430 BC; their artistic relationship is clear, but there are technical differences between them.

• Statue B was damaged and restored; in its second state (we cannot tell if this was true of its first state), it closely resembles A, as if a conscious attempt had been made to make the statues complement each other.

• The damage and the repairs must

have occurred between c. 430 BC, when statue B was made, and Nero's reign.

If one must indulge in some archaeology-fiction, a genre that has enjoyed great success with reference to these two statues, it is on the Agora in Athens that all this would seem to fit most appropriately of all. The moving of the heroes, which it is archaeologically sound to place in the 4th century BC, and their plunder by Sulla may provide causes or pretexts for the two characters' adventures. Other circumstances or episodes could surely be found within the chronological constraints that have been agreed upon.

Claude Rolley
Ibid.

Should the Parthenon sculptures be returned to Athens?

Has the passage of time created rights that justify keeping the marbles in London? The return of the Elgin Marbles to Athens would not pose so many problems if the great museums of the world did not all fear that they could suddenly be stripped of their masterpieces because of the demands of countries where these masterpieces were found.

A complicated issue: Lord Elgin and his defence

The group of artists commissioned by Lord Elgin arrived in Athens in August 1800. Out of caution or whim, the military governor of the Acropolis demanded a firman; this authorization was obtained without too much trouble, as the British had just brought about the surrender of the French army at Cairo, and the sultan could not therefore refuse the ambassador of Great Britain anything.

Letter of the Grand Vizier to the civil governor *(voïvode)* and to the president of the tribunal *(cadi)* of Athens:

'Our wish is that, upon receipt of this

The young Lord Elgin.

letter, you should comply strictly with the requests of the said ambassador, for as long as the said five artists staying in the city shall be employed in his service, to enter and leave the fortress of Athens, or to set up scaffolding around the ancient temple of the idols, or to model the said ornaments and figures that are visible in lime or plaster, or to take down measurements of the remains of other ruined buildings, or to excavate the foundations where they judge necessary in the search for inscriptions buried beneath the rubble; and they should not be hindered, either by the said [military governor], or by any other person including yourself to whom this letter is addressed, and no person should touch their scaffolding or instruments or prevent them from removing any stone bearing inscriptions or figures.'

Did the firman authorize them to excavate and remove material they uncovered or to carry off any piece wherever it had come from, even if it was still in place on the monument? It was this second interpretation that Philip Hunt, Elgin's chaplain and secretary, got the Turkish authorities to accept.

Fourteen years later, in 1816, at the time of the purchase of the collection by Britain, a commission made inquiries about the value of the marbles and the circumstances of their removal.

Elgin defended what he had done: 'By collecting these remains of antiquity for the benefit of my country, and by saving them from future destruction, which threatened them inexorably if they had remained for many years the prey of malevolent Turks, who mutilated them for a senseless pleasure or with the aim of selling them off piece by piece to

passing travellers, I was not impelled by the search for personal gain.'

These arguments convinced public opinion. Only one voice was heard that prefigured the debates that were to come. It was the voice of Hugh Hammersley, a member of the House of Commons, who deplored the fact 'that the state did not repudiate this act of pillage' and proposed that 'Great Britain should only retain these marbles in her safekeeping until the present ruler of the city of Athens, or any future ruler, should claim them back'.

Roland Etienne

Melina Mercouri expresses the Greek point of view

About six months ago I dared to suggest that these marbles should return to Greece. Since then, a small tempest has raged. But what I found interesting was that, after an interview with the BBC, hundreds of letters from individuals and from organizations arrived from England giving me encouragement. I see in these letters the love of the English people for justice and beauty. Besides, Lord Elgin's sacrilege had immediately aroused reproach, even in England. Outraged, the Briton Edward Dodwell wrote: 'I have known the humiliation of being present at the despoiling of the Parthenon of its most brilliant sculptures and at the destruction of some magnificent architectural portions of the temple.' While Lord Byron wrote: 'When one pillages and destroys the marvels of the centuries, which time and barbary have managed to spare, no excuse may be found, whoever the author of this base destruction may be.... I am speaking objectively, I am with Greece and I do not believe that the pillage in India or

Sculptures from the pediment of the Parthenon: Dionysos, Demeter, Kore (above). Another view of the purchase of the Elgin Marbles (below).

The Elgin Marbles! or John Bull buying Stones at the time his numerous Family want Bread!!

Attica is to England's honour.'

Lord Elgin declared that his action was motivated by idealism, that these marbles had to be saved from 'uncultivated hands and indifferent minds'. Here I shall tell you a little story:

The Acropolis was occupied by Ottoman forces being besieged by the army of Greek national liberation. The Ottoman occupants of the Acropolis found themselves short of ammunition. They therefore began to destroy the columns to take the lead from them and make cannonballs from it. The Greeks sent them a message I consider to be of historic importance: 'Do not touch the columns of the Acropolis – we will send you cannonballs.' And that is what they did. It was these uncultivated hands that carried the cannonballs and these indifferent minds that gave their lives in defence of their heritage.

Our great poet Yannis Ritsos expressed the feeling of our entire people when he wrote, '*Aftes i petres den bolebontai me ligotero ourano.*' ('These stones cannot make do with less sky.')

I believe that the time has come for these marbles to return to the blue sky of Attica, to their natural place, to the place where they form a structural and functional part of a unique ensemble. All this, at a time when the Greeks, with the help and the technical collaboration of the whole world, have set up scaffolding around the Propylaia, the Erechtheion and the Parthenon, in a gigantic effort to preserve the Acropolis, which is threatened by the erosion of time and the pollution of the contemporary world.

Melina Mercouri,
Greek Minister of Culture
and Science,
speech made 29 July 1982

In defence of Lord Elgin

Lord Elgin was not alone in his own time ... in wishing to possess sculptures from the Parthenon. Others of his contemporaries, notably the French diplomats Choiseul-Gouffier and Fauvel, had the same ambition, but they lacked his means and opportunities....

Elgin sold the sculptures to the British Museum ... but made no financial gain because of the costs of payment and transport.

Yet perhaps the combined efforts of the early Christians, Morosini and Elgin have done the building less harm than that inflicted on it every day by the weather, with effects that have accumulated over the centuries. Elgin had casts made of the slabs from the west frieze, which he left in position. When the condition of these casts in 1801 is compared with the condition of the originals today the difference is horrifying. The more time passes without something being done to protect the sculptures that remain on the building, the more disapproval of Elgin's theft turns into gratitude for the fact that at least the sculptures in the British Museum have been spared further damage.

Moreover the sculptures were able to radiate a far stronger cultural influence from London than they could have done from Athens, which was extremely difficult to reach in the early nineteenth century. As the 'Elgin Marbles' they had an immense effect on the classicism of the day, on art as well as on ideas.

Frank Brommer
The Sculptures of the Parthenon, 1979

The *Venus de Milo:* is she Greek, German or French?

A jewel of the Louvre in Paris, the Venus *might just as easily have gone to Germany in the frenzied competition to pillage Greece at the beginning of the 19th century.*

The story of an abduction

It was on this island [Melos, or Milo], very probably on 8 April 1820, that the bust of the statue was discovered by chance by a Greek peasant simply called Yorgos by most of the sources, who was digging in his field not far from the remains of an ancient theatre. Digging up the ruins of a small building that was half-buried in the ground, he was looking for stones with which to build a wall. Disappointed by the irregular appearance of the block of marble, he was about to cover it up again. But, as chance would have it, he was being watched by a cadet of the French navy, Olivier Voutier, who belonged to the crew of the *Estafette;* this was a schooner in the fleet that continually crossed the waters of the eastern Mediterranean to protect French interests there. The

T he discovery of the *Venus de Milo* (from the monument to Dumont d'Urville).

A VENUS DE MILO EST TRANSBORDEE
U NAVIRE LE GALAXIDI A BORD DE
A GOELETTE L'ESTAFETTE

The *Venus de Milo* being transported.

young man was fascinated by Greek antiquity and was not averse to doing a little research with his men whenever he went ashore. He thus realized the importance of the discovery at once and encouraged the peasant, giving him a few piastres, to go on digging. It was then that the lower part of the statue appeared, with a set of disparate fragments, some of which had obviously broken off from the statue: the bun of her hair, a few pieces of drapery from around the hips. The drawing that Voutier made on the spot of the separate blocks that were discovered shows quite strikingly that the *Venus* was unearthed without her arms, whatever the stories that were later to be spread about the circumstances and conditions of the discovery. While the sailor alerted Louis Brest, the French

consular officer in Melos, the peasant, who had continued to clear the site, added more fragments to those that had already been found, including two Hermaic pillars, to which a third would later be added, pieces of arms, a mutilated hand holding a fruit and two inscribed stones. Voutier's sketch records the existence of the first two pillars, as well as of the inscriptions, in a spontaneous reconstruction, the importance of which will be discussed later. A third inscribed block, which was by itself, would enrich the discovery still further....

While Brest was still hesitating about whether to attempt to buy the statues for the French nation, one of the island's notables exerted pressure on the peasant to reserve the statue for a high Greek dignitary, Nicholas Morusi, a dragoman of the Arsenal of Constantinople and a collector of antiquities, in the hope of winning his favour, which he was, at the time, very anxious to obtain. On Voutier's insistence, the consular agent

The Marquis de Rivière.

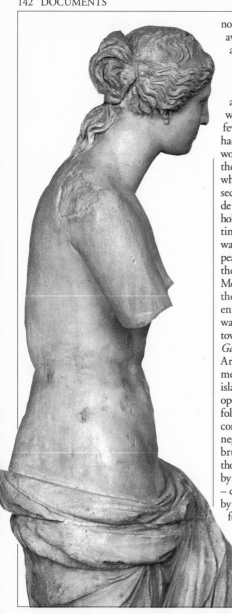

nonetheless made Yorgos promise to await the decision of the French ambassador to the [Ottoman empire], the Marquis de Rivière. He was advised, first by Dumont d'Urville, who, at the time, was an ensign on another ship of the Eastern fleet and who had been able to see the statue a few days after its discovery – but he had not shown the interest in it he would later claim to have shown – and then by Robert, captain of the vessel on which Voutier was serving. He sent a secretary from the embassy, the Comte de Marcellus, to negotiate with the holder of the find. He arrived just in time. Submitting to the pressure that was being exerted on him, the Greek peasant had come to an agreement with the representative of the dragoman Morusi. At the very moment at which the boat carrying Marcellus and Voutier entered the harbour of Melos, the statue was being moved out on a rowboat toward an 'Albanian' ship, the *Galaxidi*, which was to carry it to the Arsenal of Constantinople. The French met at once with the authorities on the island and obtained a pause in the operation. Discussions and bargaining followed. Finally, at the end of a confused series of events and of various negotiations, the deal was concluded, brutally, according to some, even though there is no solid proof of this; or by diplomacy alone, according to others – diplomacy backed up, nevertheless, by the presence of a warship. Duly paid for, the marble became the personal property of the Marquis de Rivière, and was moved directly from the *Galaxidi* onto the French boat.

Alain Pasquier
La Vénus de Milo et les Aphrodites du Louvre, 1985

The German claims

Ludwig, the heir apparent of Bavaria, had acquired the theatre of Melos in order to conduct excavations in it, and it does appear that this was where the *Venus* was discovered. At least that was the basis of the Bavarian claims to the statue.

Ludwig of Bavaria wrote to Leo von Klenze on 6 July 1821: 'I ask you urgently to write to Gau [a German architect living in Paris], so that he may give you information about the *Venus Victrix*. Where was it found – not the region but the precise spot? It is said to be the work of Phidias. To what known work may its beauty be compared? I would like to know that.'

In reply, Leo von Klenze assured Ludwig: 'The idea of being able to claim such a work for Your Majesty and for our nation makes me very happy.'

The evidence for the German claims was never produced; all that would remain of the *Venus* in Bavaria was a foot, which inspired a court sculptor to model the feet of Lola Montès, the king's mistress.

Roland Etienne

The Greeks do not demand the return of the *Venus*

We think that it is not right to ask museums to strip themselves of foreign works. We have repeated this ceaselessly. The fact is that the *Venus de Milo* is an independent piece, a statue that is complete in and of itself. The marbles of the Parthenon are part of an exceptional monument whose integrity has been broken.

Melina Mercouri
BBC interview, 13 February 1983

The *Venus de Milo* in 1871, undergoing restoration.

In 1821 the Venus *was offered to Louis XVIII, who presented it to the Louvre.*

Can archaeologists be trusted?

Nobody makes a cleverer or more dangerous forger than a good archaeologist. As early as the 15th century, Cyriacus of Ancona mixed genuine and fake antiquities. More recently, two characters stand out in this regard: Father Fourmont, at the beginning of the 18th century, and Heinrich Schliemann, in the 19th century.

A travelling priest

In 1728, in the reign of Louis XV, Father Fourmont and Father Sevin, both members of the [French] Académie des Inscriptions et Belles-Lettres, set off for Constantinople. Since the Renaissance, the tireless quest for Greek and Eastern manuscripts had relied upon the conviction of scholars that a large number of classical works lost to the West were to be found in the library of the seraglio of Constantinople, the former library of the Byzantine emperors. (It would be shown in the 19th century that the seraglio did not contain the riches it had been reputed to hold.) The enterprise ended in failure. Unable to gain admittance to the seraglio, the two scholars parted, Fourmont leaving Constantinople for Greece. His aim of 'collecting inscriptions [there] with a view to clarifying some of the circumstances of Greek history' would seem to place him in the tradition of Jacob Spon's successors, who wished to advance historical scholarship.

Father Fourmont travelled through Greece for sixteen months. In Athens and Attica, he collected a crop of inscriptions and bas-reliefs, many of which Spon had missed, as Fourmont took pleasure in pointing out. He then moved into the Peloponnese, where he 'excavated' several sites. From his correspondence, one can imagine the way in which these operations were carried out: 'I wanted to get them, above all, from Sparta; it's a quarry of inscribed marble which I was to excavate scrupulously.... I therefore put workmen to work destroying the

Heinrich Schliemann.

remains of that superb city, right down to its foundations, and, today, not one stone remains upon another.'

These remarks were no doubt prompted by boastfulness and by the need to justify to his superiors the expenses of a project that he had not been authorized to undertake: 'The destruction was, in the absence of books, the only means of making a trip, about which so much noise had been made, truly famous.'

Just how far did his destructive zeal go? The Briton Edward Dodwell heard stories at Mistra seventy years later about this Frenchman who, after copying the inscriptions, smashed them to pieces, destroying once and for all the traces of the past.

Fourmont returned to France claiming to have collected 2600 inscriptions; even if, as appears to be the case, he really obtained only half of that number, the booty was considerable. The Comte de Caylus, one of the great antique dealers of the century, published them and the bas-reliefs of Laconia (Sparta, Amyclae), in all good faith. It was not until half a century later that the Englishman Richard Payne Knight (Lord Elgin's famous critic and, quite apart from that, a remarkable Hellenist) proved that the lists of princes, magistrates and priests of Sparta were obvious forgeries. Lord Aberdeen revealed another deception with respect to a sculpted relief: where Fourmont had seen and reproduced blades and limbs – the evidence of human sacrifices in Laconia – these were actually merely washing and grooming instruments, dedicated to feminine divinities. This was all it took to discredit totally the whole of Fourmont's work. In fact, however, as

contemporary research has shown, a substantial portion of that work deserves to be rehabilitated. People still wonder what reasons may have caused Fourmont to manufacture fakes. It is clear that at the end of his mission his psychological state was somewhat unbalanced and that, before returning to France, he became obsessed by the need to announce that he had made some sensational discoveries; and since, in his own eyes, he had not, in fact, made any, he proceeded to fabricate some. In the end, his deception did not do him any good at all, since by an irony of fate the authentic documents were never published during his lifetime.

Françoise Etienne

Aspects of Schliemann's personality

The controversy around Schliemann has still not subsided altogether. If the voices of those who originally opposed him so firmly have been silent for a long time, from time to time one still hears, especially from those who are strangers to archaeology, the hymns of praise of those who blindly idealize Schliemann and celebrate in him the ideal of the scholar. Today, one can judge his merits and failings calmly, to the extent to which these are discernible to scholarship, and one can form an unbiased judgment that will be acceptable at least to those who judge archaeological questions in a scientific manner....

Schliemann's achievement was nothing less than to have rediscovered a buried world, which preceded all that had been known until that time.... The world of learning will be forever in Schliemann's debt for this undeniable and inestimable service; his name is forever linked to the Homeric world.

People will also remember the noble Greek woman who so generously shared with her husband all the worries and troubles, but also the successes and the glory that he experienced....

Yet there is another side to this brilliant coin. In his attitudes, as in his entire training, Schliemann remained a stranger to all scientific ways of thinking and methodology. He did not have a sense of history or art, as is revealed by the indifference he showed toward Praxiteles' Hermes: distant epochs, curious objects, vague images, exhausted his interest. He was, in fact, a dilettante in the full sense of the word – in the positive sense, a man who was passionate about his hobby, but also in the negative sense, a man who pursued his aims without a method and without basic knowledge. He was also a dilettante where excavations were concerned; he had no inkling that there might be a rigorous method and technique; he was a dilettante in matters of architecture and archaeology.

Adolf Michaelis
Archaeological Discoveries of the Nineteenth Century, 1906

Schliemann, dilettante and psychopath

Like many men of genius, Schliemann had much psychopathy in his personality. He lived or acted some of it out in his behaviour. An unhappy childhood had led to prolonged infantilism. This is apparent in his lifelong obsessive writing of autobiographies and his endless composing of letters to famous people. If they remained in his [estate], how many did he actually send? I should add another remarkable and neglected piece of evidence. In the cemetery at Ankershagen, a large cross stands to the right of the church as seen from the west. [Marking his mother's grave,] it bears this inscription [in German]:

HENRY SCHLIEMANN
IN ST PETERSBURG,
TO HIS BELOVED MOTHER
LOUISE THERESE SOPHIA
SCHLIEMANN, BORN CITIZEN
18 MAY 1793, DIED 22 MARCH 1831

The anglicized Christian name, his name before that of his mother, the inclusion of his domicile at St Petersburg on an inscription at Ankershagen – all these details make the cross rather a monument for Schliemann himself than for his mother.

A lack of conscience may have been acquired from his father. This fortunate endowment made him a successful businessman. He would not hesitate a moment to deceive a colleague. He was an eager war profiteer, whether from the Crimean War or the American Civil War. A dream on 17 March 1855 inspired him to corner the saltpetre market and win a fortune from the Crimean War. This same lack of conscience made him a successful archaeologist. The Turkish government forbade him to excavate Hissarlik. He excavated Hissarlik. The owners of the property forbade him to excavate their hill. He excavated it. The Turkish government forbade him to export his finds. He smuggled them to Athens. In a letter to Queen Sophie of Holland, presenting her with a gift of twelve ancient figurines, he informs her that the package cannot be sent 'by the direct steamer, the exportation of antiquities being strictly prohibited in Greece'. He treated governments like business rivals....

Schliemann's house, Athens.

How did his psychopathy affect his archaeology? The disinterested recording of finds, their description, the drawings, need not be universally doubted. Much can be controlled by the extant objects themselves. Rather, specific interpretation must be queried and often discarded. The fantasy life of his diaries and letters became the fantasy life of his excavation reports. A Roman glass vessel found at Ithaca contains the ashes of Odysseus. A Bronze Age treasure becomes the jewelry of the fair Helen. A nameless mummy is the corpse of King Agamemnon. The minister at Athens learns by cable of Schliemann's discovery of 'the dead man with the round face. This one is very like the picture which my imagination formed of Agamemnon long ago'. Again Schliemann makes fact. An exultant telegram to the king of Greece follows. A secretary replied.

A critical investigation of Schliemann's autobiography remains a pressing task. We must doubt every statement in any autobiographical document composed by Schliemann, unless an external control can be adduced to confirm it.

William M. Calder III
'Schliemann on Schliemann:
A Study on the Use of Sources',
Greek, Roman and Byzantine Studies,
1972

Philip II, king of Macedon: his flesh and bones

In 1977 Professor Manolis Andronikos of the University of Salonika made one of the most spectacular discoveries of the last fifteen years. He found the tomb of Philip II, king of Macedon (359–336 BC), the father of Alexander the Great.

Entrance to the tomb of Philip II of Macedon.

The excitement of the discovery

The keystone of the vault was removed with little effort. It left an opening about a foot wide; it was sufficient, first, to look inside, and then to go down on a wooden ladder. At first, I kept looking at the other side of the marble door that separated the main chamber from the vestibule and then at the walls. At that moment, my first reaction was of intense disappointment. The door had a rough, badly worked surface. The walls were undecorated; they were not even painted, and it was clear that they had not even received the slightest finishing coat, which is carefully applied to stuccoed buildings in Macedon. But the shock was almost immediate when my gaze fell to the floor of the chamber. In a preliminary official report I tried rapidly to outline my state of mind at that moment. I wrote: 'This is not the place to relate what goes through the excavator's mind at this exceptional moment of his archaeological career. The reader may imagine that whereas one had to remain cool, calm and

M etal vases, tripod and shield from the tomb, at the time of their discovery.

collected in order to assume the responsibilities imposed by the situation, the digger was profoundly troubled and amazed at the sight of the riches of a funerary chamber that had remained intact for centuries, from the moment when the marble doors had been shut following the final funerary rites. The long years spent studying funerary customs, far from deadening his sensibility, had heightened it to such a point that he experienced moments of intense emotion which can never be felt again, when he was able thus to cross thousands of years and to touch the living truth of the past, as though in a direct experience. The researcher felt the exaltation of a scholar and the remorse of a profaner; naturally, the first emotion was stronger than the second.

'My eyes were fixed upon the rear portion of the chamber, directly below the opening. There were heaped all the objects provided for the deceased's life beyond the grave. To my right, in the southwestern corner of his chamber, there were piles of bronze and iron objects; the bronze pieces had acquired a fine, dark-green patina through oxidation. Those made of iron had turned black. On the left, near the north wall, shone silver vessels. In the centre of the back wall, just below our opening, there was the square stone cover of a marble sarcophagus; beside it, in front of us, lay the sparse remains of blackened wood that had decayed and disintegrated but amid which sparkled some small fragments; golden leaves shone all over this area. Beyond them was the oxidized red-and-black breast-plate. The rest of the floor was bare.'

Manolis Andronikos
Vergina, The Royal Tombs, 1984

Medicine comes to the aid of archaeology

I am satisfied that [these] bones do display a number of anatomical peculiarities and asymmetries that need not be attributed to the effects of fire. [The body of Philip II had been burned and the remains carefully placed in a golden chest, or larnax.] The latter should not of course be ruled out altogether, as it remains impossible to predict precisely what will happen to any given bone on exposure to very high temperatures. However, I feel more inclined to attribute them to trauma, congenital abnormality, or a combination of both. Support for this hypothesis was given to [us] by the experienced plastic and oral surgeons to whom we showed casts and photographs in Manchester and Bristol. If nature rather than fire really was the culprit, then the suggestion that the bones belonged to a man known to have lost his right eye and perhaps sustained major injuries to much of the right side of his face eighteen years before his death becomes very attractive indeed.

Jonathan H. Musgrave
Journal of Hellenic Studies, 1984

The discovery of Greece by means of the plaster cast

It is not enough to make discoveries; one must also make these discoveries known. Classical culture was made familiar to large numbers of people by means of plaster casts that were made of famous antiquities. Starting in the 16th century, they appeared beside originals in museum collections.

Some schools of fine arts and universities formed collections of plaster casts for their educational value. Nowadays, audiovisual resources appear to have made them obsolete. It is nevertheless worthwhile to preserve this important cultural heritage. Today, the museum at Lyons has been transformed into offices and classrooms.

The old museum of Lyons

It was in 1893 that the French minister of education and the fine arts (the second part of his title is often forgotten) decided to establish a museum of plaster casts of antiquities on the second floor of the university buildings in Lyons, which were under construction at the time. The museum was opened in 1899, and most of the collections were already present. How much the buildings cost to put up is

The pediment from Aegina and the Tyrannicide Group (in the foreground), from the old Museum of Plaster Casts at the University of Lyons–II.

not known, but Henri Lechat, the museum's first curator, estimated the value of the collections to be 100,000 French francs in 1903. At current value, the replacement cost of the casts would be as high as 13 million francs ($2.5 million). Nevertheless, I do not wish to stress the value of the collection but to describe instead the creation of a museum of plaster casts at the turn of the century.

It should be emphasized, first, how exciting the formation of such a gathering of collections from the museums of Austria, Greece, Italy and Great Britain must have been.

The Lyons museum grew with the purchase of new casts as excavations revealed new masterpieces. The frieze of the Treasury of Siphnos was discovered in Delphi in 1893; it was mentioned in the *Bulletin de Correspondance Hellénique* in 1894, and by 1895 there was a cast of it in Lyons; it is mentioned in a letter at that time from a scholar who was responsible for the creation of the museum. The Sphinx of the Naxians arrived a little later. (Certain parts of it were already known, but its head was not discovered until 1894.) The cast was exhibited at the Universal Exposition in 1900 and then presented to the museum in Lyons. The museum thus reflected the amazing expansion of archaeology in the 1890s and 1900s. It is not surprising that there are so many of the korai from the Acropolis in Lyons when one considers that Henri Lechat

was an expert on archaic Greek art. As a young member of the French School at Athens, he described the discoveries made on the Acropolis as early as 1888; its systematic excavation had finally been begun by Kavvadias in 1885. The Lyons museum followed the news and publicized all the new aspects of a Greek culture whose extraordinary diversity was being discovered in the 1900s. Such a museum was looked upon as a model; E. Pottier confirmed this last point when explaining why he awarded the gold medal of the Universal Exposition to the museum in 1900: 'The jury wished to present the museum to the other universities as a model and to set it very clearly apart from and above its competitors.'

The museum covered 1600 square metres on the second floor of the Faculty of Arts and Law. The statues and reliefs were arranged in historical order in ten large rooms, one of which was an imposing rotunda that held the pieces from the 5th century BC. The ceilings were six to seven metres high, the lighting was by means of skylights; in short, the best technical solutions available to display problems were used. In order to avoid the monotony of uniformly smooth partitions, the architect had divided the space up into small cabinets. The ends of the walls that separated them were adorned with painted gray columns that stood out from the Pompeian red walls. A neoclassical style of presentation had been chosen, and the shiny wooden floor helped to give the museum the appearance of a collector's home.

Roland Etienne
'Le Nouveau Musée de Moulages de l'Université de Lyon–II', (Proceedings of the International Conference of 10–12 April 1987), in *Le Moulage*, 1988

Scenes from the Lyons museum.

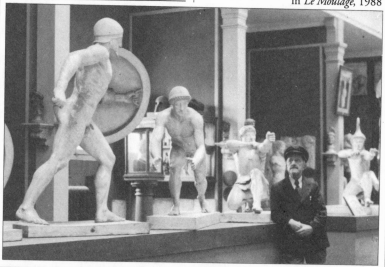

Save the Acropolis!

The most famous Greek ruin, the Acropolis in Athens, is at the centre of an impassioned and fascinating dispute. The use of sophisticated techniques, the extent of financial resources and the place of the ruin in the contemporary urban fabric are all hotly debated.

Avoiding a catastrophe

Until the year 2000, the sacred rock of the Acropolis will continue to give the impression of a great building site that is covered with scaffolding, machinery and workers, an image that may not be very different from that presented by the Acropolis at the time of Pericles, when our ancestors created this unique monumental ensemble. It is an image that cannot be avoided today, for it is only in this way that the superb monuments of the ancient world that are the heritage not only of the Greeks but of the entire human race will be

The east facade of the Parthenon in the course of restoration.

preserved for centuries to come....

While the monuments of the Acropolis have, for almost 2500 years, resisted natural disasters, human interventions and the natural process of aging, in the last decades, especially since 1940, they have experienced serious problems: fractures, cracks and the alteration of the surface of the marble.

In 1971 a report by experts at UNESCO stressed the gravity of the situation. It is true that the *ephory* [a division of the Greek Archaeological Service] of the Acropolis (Ministry of Culture), with the limited technical and financial means at its disposal, has attempted to find an answer to the question of the possibility of immediate catastrophe. In 1975, it was fully acknowledged that serious measures would have to be taken in order to save the monuments. That was why a commission, made up of archaeologists, architects, engineers and chemists, was set up at the Ministry of Culture; this was the 'Commission for the Conservation of the Monuments of the Acropolis', whose mission is still to study, plan, supervise and execute the work that is needed to restore the entire monumental complex.

To implement this plan, immediately upon its formation, the commission created a technical panel composed of scholars from different fields. The really important work thus began barely twelve years ago; its cost will amount to

The Parthenon undergoing restoration.

several thousand million drachmas [1 thousand million drachmas = approximately £3 million]! The first grants, which became available in 1977 through an international pool established by UNESCO, were used to set up a laboratory for the conservation of marble. Later, especially between 1983 and 1985, the European Economic Community made a partial contribution. But these were still only small amounts. Since 1985, the financial burden of the work has been borne by the Ministry of Culture. The restoration work is being carried out by Greek scholars. The team consists of six architects, three engineers, three chemists, three archaeologists, five draftsmen, a restorer and various technicians specializing in marble.

As was reported in the press release that the commission published recently, the period from 1975 to 1977 was the real study phase of the project. In these years, an inventory of the problems that had been studied in depth was carefully drawn up. The most important of these were:

a) the corrosion of the pieces of iron that were used in the restorations of the 19th and 20th centuries;

b) the alteration (physical, chemical, biological) that has occurred in the surface of the marble as a result of the sudden increase in atmospheric pollution in the immediate environment of the monuments over the last thirty years;

c) the static resistance of the monuments; and

d) the deterioration of the rock due to the passage of thousands of visitors.

The commission of the Acropolis, with the assistance of other scholarly teams, has overseen the progress in static research on all the buildings, the topographic and graphic study of the rock and the study of the blocks that have been dispersed. In addition, the state of the rock of the Acropolis has been studied systematically, and research has been done in the laboratory on the causes of the alteration in the surface of the marble. At the same time, preliminary measures have been taken to protect the monuments, such as covering the balustrade of the caryatids and the west frieze of the Parthenon with a wooden roof, transferring the sculptures of the west pediment of the Parthenon to the Acropolis Museum and installing them in a place affording them special conditions, enacting measures to clean the air, and banning visitors from entering the monuments and cars from driving up to the base of the Acropolis. The first phase was concluded at the end of 1977.

The first important monument in need of restoration was the Erechtheion. Restoration work began in 1979 and was completed at the end of 1986. The entire monument was dismantled and reassembled after various measures that were judged vital had been taken....

In 1983 'The Study for the Restoration of the Parthenon' was published by the leading architects M. Korre and C. Bouras. In this study, it was proposed, among other things, that scattered fragments of the monument should be moved back to their rightful places on the Parthenon and that wherever it was deemed necessary, the parts of the monument that had been destroyed should be replaced with new marble.

Karolos Moraitis
Vradyni, 9 November 1987

Should the Erechtheion be reconstructed?

Where should the restoration of ancient monuments stop? Sir Arthur Evans' reconstruction at Knossos has been widely criticized for being based on insufficiently reliable scholarly grounds and for being irreversible. Should there be no reconstruction? Does it make sense to leave buildings in a state in which they remain incomprehensible to the general public, merely in the name of scholarship?

The Porch of the Caryatids of the Erechtheion before restoration.

Daring or conservative?

What is one to make of the restoration of the Erechtheion that was completed at the end of 1987, after eight years of study and work? The debate about the restored appearance, which finally determined the measures taken on the monument, is not new. Yet disagreements had not previously surfaced outside the meetings of the

Commission of the Acropolis, scholarly papers or private debates. Today, for the first time, they are exposed to the public and, moreover, appear in the pages of the British press.

In a recent letter to *The Times* [of London], which he sent from Athens, the archaeologist Georges Dontas, the former director of the Acropolis and a member of the commission, claimed that the principles of the Venice Charter (the Charter of Venice, 1964, is a set of international rules governing the restoration of monuments), the bible of restoration, had been violated and the intervention had gone too far. In the main, this opinion is held by the old guard of archaeologists in Greece and abroad, which states that the monuments should be preserved and protected from additional catastrophe but that the form they had at the time of their discovery should be maintained. The opposite view is defended by a full-page article in the *Sunday Times* of two days ago, in which

Simon Jenkins maintains that the restorers of the Erechtheion 'have been the prisoners of academic timidity'. He goes on to write that 'the Acropolis of the future will be a mausoleum of archaeological conservatism', and ends with these words: 'How fascinating if just one of the Periclean monuments could break free from archaeology's intellectual monopoly and have its glory restored to it: a majestic, garish celebration of the pagan gods. Our antagonism to such reconstruction is perverse. Lulled by an affection for the picturesque, we appear afraid to come face to face with the realism of the past.'

Midway between these two conflicting viewpoints lies the solution that was finally adopted.… Its principle is a balance between the two theses and the decision to pursue the restoration for as long as there is any material left, even if that material is in the British Museum, as in the case of the sixth column of the northeast corner of the building. The empty space in the monument has been filled with a copy. (Dontas, as well as the director of the restoration at the Ministry of Culture, I. Demakopoulos, disagreed with this particular decision.)

Yet Jenkins asks for something more than the addition of a column, the completion with new marble, the repositioning of scattered blocks and the morphological continuity which has been restored to the Erechtheion. The British journalist puts forward the view that the monuments have to be made comprehensible to the general public. To explain his thesis, he adds: 'Great buildings (such as Knossos, the

Cathedral of Chartres, etc.) live and breathe through those who seek to restore to them some of their old meaning, not those who seek merely to place one stone correctly on another.' He adds: 'The half-restoration of the present Erechtheion is no more true than a full restoration might have been …the latter at least true to the original architect's intentions.' On this point, Jenkins gives as an example the work done by the American School on the Stoa of Attalos. (The Stoa of Attalos is a portico that was built in the ancient Agora of Athens by the King of Pergamum, Attalos II, in c. 150 BC. The monument was completely rebuilt by the Americans in 1953–6 and is used as a museum. The original blocks are displayed in cases.) 'Modern archaeology and technology could enable us to restore to Pericles' Acropolis masterpieces their former meaning and glory.… We can respect the character of the original buildings. All that would go would be their ruins, the arbitrary creations of historical chance.'

The forty-five-year-old Jenkins takes an active part in restoration and is a member of several committees concerned with monuments in Britain.… His article has aroused favourable reactions in Greece; yet the decision that was taken to maintain a balance has remained in force. This solution respects the archaeological view by adding to the architectural components of a monument only where it is strictly necessary. It does not conceal the character of the ruins, and it does help the ordinary citizen who is unfamiliar with the archaeological findings to understand the beauty of the monument.

The statues and architecture of the Erechtheion are badly deteriorated.

Ta Nea, 5 January 1988

Should further excavations be undertaken?

Anthony Snodgrass, a professor at Cambridge University, is one of the most eminent representatives of British archaeology. His work dealing with the early ages of Greece up to archaic times is authoritative. Here he boldly chooses to tackle a fundamental question that may well open, or reopen, a wide-ranging debate.

Objects from the excavation of the Agora in Athens.

The form of future archaeological work in Greece

I have referred in passing to the difficulties under which the Greek Archaeological Service labours, and I hope that it will not seem too presumptuous to enlarge on them a little. The unselective preservation of Greece's material heritage, which is a cause so estimable in principle that almost nobody would speak in public against it, has brought about another, less obvious, crisis. The historically conscious visitor to Greece today is rightly impressed by the steady increase in the number of local museums and in the quality of exhibition. What he or she may not appreciate – and I think that this is true even of classicists and

other 'professionals' who are not archaeologists – is that what is actually displayed is merely the beautiful tip of an unsightly iceberg. Almost every museum in Greece is compelled to conceal in its storerooms a mass, growing year by year at an alarming pace, of material unsuited to exhibition, which is often unpublished and sometimes destined to remain so. If the Archaeological Service were rewarded, either in salaries or in manpower, on a scale that bore some faint relation to the colossal indirect contribution that its activities make to the nation's tourist industry, then one could look ahead to a possible reduction of the pressure. As things are, the only prospect is that it will rapidly increase: even to keep pace with the rate of growth in the 'submerged nine-tenths' of its holdings, the service would need an increase in manpower. Much of the

material has to be stored in improvised accommodation, difficult of access for study; meanwhile, its keepers are distracted by the ever more persistent demands of emergency excavation....

The activities of the foreign missions in Greece make a contribution towards shouldering one of the burdens, through their undertaking rescue excavations when asked. But, since they must necessarily share the same museum facilities, they inevitably aggravate the other main burden by adding to the growth of the unseen '*apotheke* [storeroom] mountain'. The problem is not peculiar to Greece but, because of the exceptional richness of Greece's archaeological heritage, it appears there in its acutest form. Any excavation, even that of a ten-metre square undertaken to prepare the way for the building of a modest office block in a provincial town, is likely to produce a significant crop of material from a variety of periods, spanning millennia rather than centuries. Some answer to the problem has to be found in the near future. The option of a total moratorium on all but emergency excavations, which used to exist only in the context of examination papers of classical students, begins to move in the direction of serious possibility. It is time to ask ourselves whether our appetite for new objects, connoted by the invocation '*Kala vremata!*' ('Good finds!'), which is still regularly heard at international gatherings of archaeologists, is something that can be allowed to be satisfied indefinitely. Can it not, perhaps, be separated from the appetite, entirely justifiable and indeed desirable, for new knowledge?

Anthony Snodgrass
An Archaeology of Greece, 1987

Ancient Greece
(5000 BC–AD 395)

Neolithic 5000–2600 BC	Aegean-Anatolian civilization
Bronze Age 2600–1000 BC	**c. 1950–c. 1750 BC** In Knossos, Crete, the first Minoan palace. On the mainland, the arrival of the Greeks
	c. 1580–c. 1400 BC In Crete, the second Minoan palaces. On the mainland, the development of Mycenaean civilization
	c. 1500 BC Eruption of the volcano on Santorini, destruction of the site of Akrotiri
	c. 1400–c. 1100 BC Conquest of Crete by the Mycenaeans, peak of the Mycenaean civilization
	c. 1250 BC The Trojan War (traditional date: 1184 BC)
	c. 1200–1125 BC Mycenaean palaces destroyed
Iron Age from c. 1100 BC	Invasion of the Dorians. Period of transition. The birth of Geometric art
Hellenic Period 776–323 BC	**c. 776 BC** Founding of the Olympic Games (traditional date)
	c. 750 BC Founding of Cumae, the first Greek colony in Asia Minor
	From 750 BC Greek colonization in the West
	499–478 BC War between the Greeks and the Persians
	c. 448–432 BC Parthenon built under Pericles
	431–404 BC Peloponnesian War
	390–346 BC Macedonia unified. Major cities of Chalcidian League conquered
	338 BC Defeat of the Greek city-states by Philip II of Macedon
	336 BC Philip II of Macedon killed
	336–323 BC Reign of Alexander the Great. Conquest of Persia and the Near East
Hellenistic Period c. 323–c. 30 BC	**323 BC** Alexander the Great dies
	148 BC Roman annexation of Macedonia
	146 BC Rome destroys Carthage
	88–86 BC Siege and destruction of Athens by Sulla
Period of the Roman Empire 31 BC–AD 395	**31 BC** Victory of Octavian, the future Emperor Augustus, over Antony at the battle of Actium (western Greece)
	29 BC Strabo travels to Greece and in the empire
	c. AD 150 Pausanias travels to Greece
	AD 268 The Herulians devastate Athens
	AD 395 Christianity becomes the state religion

Byzantine and Frankish Greece (395–1455 AD)		Greece under Turkish domination (1456–1820 AD)	
Historical events	**History of archaeology**	**Historical events**	**History of archaeology**
395 Division of the Roman empire into two parts: the western Roman empire and the eastern Roman (Byzantine) empire		**1456** The Turks capture Athens	**2nd half of the 15th century** Accelerated emigration of Greek scholars to the West. A renewal of the ancient arts in Greece (the teaching of the Neoplatonic philosopher Gemistus Plethon at Mistra)
529 Justinian closes philosophical schools	**529** Parthenon, 'Theseion' and other temples are made into churches	**1460** The Parthenon is given over to the Islamic faith. Turks conquer the Morea (except for the Venetian possessions)	
6th–9th centuries Invasion of the Slavs		**16th century** New Ottoman expansion, which the Venetians try, unsuccessfully, to check	
867–1081 Macedonian dynasty in Byzantium: Hellenic golden age			**1520–66** Suleiman rules the Ottoman empire, at height of its power
1054 Schism: break between the Roman Catholic Church and the Eastern Orthodox Church		**1566** The conquest of Chios, the Cyclades and Cyprus	
1204 The Fourth Crusade, the taking of Constantinople and founding of the Latin Empire of Constantinople. Partition of Greece between Venice (Ionian Islands, Aegean Islands, Rhodes, Crete, outposts of the Peloponnese) and the Frankish princes (Duchy of Athens, principality of the Morea)	**1204** Exodus of Greek scholars to the West (especially Italy)	**1571** Battle of Lepanto (Gulf of Corinth): a coalition of Christian powers (Venice, Spain and the Papal States) destroys the Turkish fleet	
		17th century Venetian-Turkish wars	**17th century** Religious orders are implanted in Greece (Capuchins and Jesuits)
		1645–69 The Turks occupy the whole of the Greek territory (including Crete)	**1674** Visit of the Marquis de Nointel, drawings of the sculptures of the Parthenon
		1687 Capture of Athens by the Venetians, led by Morosini, conquerer of the Peloponnese. Bombardment of the Parthenon	
1261 The Byzantine emperor, Michael VIII, the Palaeologus, retakes Constantinople		**18th century** Russo-Turkish Wars. Many uprisings by the Greeks, all of which end in failure	**1733** Founding of the Society of Dilettanti in London
1262 Mistra, Monemvasia and Maina are retaken	**1435–48** Voyages of Cyriacus of Ancona to Greece		**1788** Appearance of the *Voyage of the Young Anacharsis to Greece* by Father Barthélemy
1453 Fall of Constantinople to the Turks; end of the Byzantine empire			

CONTINUED ON NEXT PAGE

Greece under Turkish Domination
(1456–1820 AD)

CONTINUED FROM PREVIOUS PAGE

Historical events	History of archaeology
	1800–5 Lord Elgin in Athens
	1811 Discovery of the pediments of Aegina
1814 Founding, in Odessa, of the Hetaery, or Philiki Etaireia, a secret, revolutionary society preparing the War of Liberation	**1812** Excavations at Bassae and discovery of the frieze
	1820 Discovery and purchase of the *Venus de Milo* by France

The War of Independence
(1821–9 AD)

Historical events	History of archaeology
March 1821 Rebellion of Greece against the Turks. First Greek successes in the Peloponnese and in the islands	**1821** Creation of a powerful philhellenic movement in Europe
1822 Proclamation of the independence of the Greek nation at Epidauros. Greek reversals and massacres of Chios. Start of the siege of Missolonghi by the Turks	
1823 Civil war in Greece opposing the military party and the politicians	**1823** Creation of the London Greek Committee
1824 Death of Lord Byron at Missolonghi	**1824** Creation of the French philhellenic committee
1825 Landing in the Morea of Turko-Egyptian troops, led by Ibrahim Pasha, with the aim of subjugating Greece	

Historical events	History of archaeology
1826 Capture of Missolonghi. The Turks retake Athens and the Acropolis	
1827 Ioánnis Kapodístrias, president of the Greek republic. Mediation to bring about the end of hostilities. After Turkey's refusal, British, French and Russians sink the Turko-Egyptian fleet: battle of Navarino (southwest Peloponnese)	**1828** A scholarly expedition accompanies a French military expedition to the Morea
1829 Creation of an independent Greek state, bounded to the north by the gulfs of Volos and Arta	
1831 Assassination of Kapodístrias	
1832 The powers impose a monarchy on Greece. Otho of Bavaria installs himself in Nauplia	

Contemporary Greece
(from 1833 AD)

Historical events	History of archaeology
1833 Athens becomes capital of Greece	**1834** Greek Archaeological Service organized. The Acropolis is cleared of recent buildings
	1835 Reconstruction of the Temple of Athena Nike

Historical events	History of archaeology
1843 Revolution in Athens. Otho grants a constitution	**1837** Greek Archaeological Society founded. Opening of the University of Athens
1862 Anarchy and decline of the Bavarian dynasty	**1846** French School of Athens founded
1863–1913 Reign of George I, a Danish prince	
1864 The Ionian Islands are ceded to Greece by Great Britain	
1868 Failure of the insurrection in Crete against the Turks	**1866–89** National Archaeological Museum built in Athens. German Institute of Athens founded
1881 Treaty of Constantinople: transfer of Thessaly and part of Epiros to Greece	**1882** American Archaeological School founded
	1885 British Archaeological School founded
	1896 First modern Olympic Games
1908 Crete proclaims its union with Greece	**1909** Italian School of Archaeology founded
1912–3 Balkan Wars: Greece recovers southern Epiros and Macedonia, as well as most of the Aegean Islands	
1913 King George assassinated	
1917 Greece enters the First World War on the side of the Allies. The peace treaties give Greece Thrace, except for Constantinople and the region of Smyrna	
1921–2 Greco-Turkish War in Asia Minor leads to loss of Smyrna. Exodus of Greek refugees from Asia Minor	

Historical events	History of archaeology
1922 Revolution and fall of the monarchy	
1924–35 Proclamation of the republic	**1931** Americans excavate the Agora in Athens
1935–6 Restoration of the monarchy under King George II and dictatorship by General Ioánnis Metaxas	
1941–4 Occupation of Greece by German and Italian troops	
1944–9 Civil war in Greece	
1946 Return of King George II	
1947 The Dodecanese ceded to Greece by Italy	
1949–67 Period of instability	
1967 Military coup d'état and dictatorship	
1974 Greek troops invade Cyprus. Reestablishment of democracy in Greece. KonstantinosKaramanlis becomes premier	**1977** Discovery of the tomb of Philip II, king of Macedon
1981 Andreas Papandreou elected premier	**1979–87** Restoration of the Erechtheion

FURTHER READING

Boardman, John, *Greek Art*, 1983
—, *Greek Sculpture: The Archaic Period*, 1978
—, *Greek Sculpture: The Classical Period*, 1987
—, *The Parthenon and its Sculptures*, 1985
Browning, Robert, *The Greek World: Classical, Byzantine and Modern*, 1985
Carpenter, Thomas H., *Art and Myth in Ancient Greece*, 1991
Chadwick, John, *The Decipherment of Linear B*, 1967
Cook, B. F., *The Elgin Marbles*, 1984
—, *Greek and Roman Art in the British Museum*, 1976
Hauser, Caroline, *Greek Monumental Bronze Sculpture*, 1983
Kerény, C., *The Gods of the Greeks*, 1974
—, *The Heroes of the Greeks*, 1974
Luce, John V., *An Introduction to Greek Philosophy*, 1992
Musgrave, Jonathan H., in *Journal of Hellenic Studies*, vol. CIV, 1984
Snodgrass, Anthony M., *An Archaeology of Greece*, 1987
Starr, Chester G., *The Ancient Greeks*, 1971
Tsigakou, Fani-Maria, *The Rediscovery of Greece: Travellers and Painters of the Romantic Era*, 1981

LIST OF ILLUSTRATIONS

The following abbreviations have been used: *a* above; *b* below; *c* centre; *l* left; *r* right; BM British Museum; BN Bibliothèque Nationale; EBA Ecole des Beaux Arts, Paris; FAS French Archaeological School, Athens; GAS Greek Archaeological Society, Athens; RIBA Royal Institute of British Architects, London

COVER

Front Victor Laloux. Detail of restored transverse section through the Temple of Zeus at Olympia. Watercolour, 1883. EBA
Spine Albert Tournaire. Reconstruction of the Monument of the Naxians. Watercolour, 1894. EBA
Back Battle between Greeks and Amazons. Frieze from the Temple of Apollo at Bassae. BM

OPENING

1 Sphinx found at Delphi. Photograph. FAS
2–3 Excavations at the Heraion of Samos. Photograph, 1902. GAS
4–5 Copy of the *Diadumenos*. Delos. Photo FAS
6–7 Discovery of an archaic kouros at Delphi. Photo, 1893. FAS
8 Sir Arthur J. Evans at Knossos. Photo. Ashmolean Museum, Oxford
9 Measuring a column of the tholos at Delphi. FAS

11 Alfred Beaumont. The Choregic Monument of Lysikrates. Drawing, 1834. Museum of the City of Athens

CHAPTER 1

12 Frontispiece of the *Description of Greece* by Pausanias, late 15th century. Biblioteca Laurenziana, Florence
13 Head of the *Doryphoros*. Roman bronze after Polyclitos, Villa dei Papyri in Herculaneum. National Archaeological Museum, Naples
14 Athena Promachos. Roman, marble. *Ibid.*
15*a* Danaid. Bronze sculpture from the Villa dei Papyri in Herculaneum. *Ibid.*
15*b* Hermes resting. Bronze sculpture from the Villa dei Papyri in Herculaneum. *Ibid.*
16–7 J. Rigaud. *The Hippodrome of Olympia.* Engraving in *Pausanias or the Historical Voyage of Greece*, Paris, 1731
18–9 Map of Greece by Patrick Mérienne

CHAPTER 2

20 Map of Leukas, in Cristoforo Buondelmonti, *Liber Insularum Archipelagi*, 1420. BN
21 Cyriacus of Ancona. Statue from the Hiera Boule of Thasos. Drawing. Bodleian Library, Oxford
22–3 The port of Methoni. Coloured engraving in Bernhard von Breytenbach, *Voyage to the Holy Land*, 1486. BN
24–5 Greek islands, in Cristoforo Buondelmonti, *Liber Insularum Archipelagi*, 1420. BN
25*b* Bust of Athena signed by Eutyches. Intaglio. Museum of Antiquities, Berlin
26 Cyriacus of Ancona. The Muses. Drawing. Bodleian Library, Oxford
27 Cyriacus of Ancona. Sketches, 1445. Delos
28*a* Cyriacus of Ancona. The Parthenon, west façade. Drawing
28*b* Cyriacus of Ancona. Bust of Aristotle. Drawing. Bodleian Library, Oxford
29 Cyriacus of Ancona. Archaic Hermes on Delos. Drawing

CHAPTER 3

30 Jacques Carrey. The Parthenon frieze. Red chalk drawing, 1674. BN
31 Jacob Spon. Greek head. Drawing, 1678. BN
32*a* Turkish army at the siege of Lemnos in 1478. Drawing in the Cigogna Manuscript, c. 1600. Museo Correr, Venice
32*b* Greek nobleman. Engraving in Nicolas de Nicolay, *Les Quatre Premiers Livres des Navigations et Pérégrinations Orientales*, 1568
33*a* Woman from the island of Chios. *Ibid.*

INDEX

Figures in italics refer to pages on which captions appear.